ALSO BY TOM SILEO

Fire in My Eyes:
*An American Warrior's Journey from Being Blinded on the
Battlefield to Gold Medal Victory* (with Brad Snyder)

Brothers Forever:
*The Enduring Bond Between a Marine and a Navy SEAL That
Transcended Their Ultimate Sacrifice* (with Tom Manion)

A SOLDIER'S STORY

FROM IMMIGRANT

TO THE

MEDAL OF HONOR

8 SECONDS OF COURAGE

FLO GROBERG

AND

TOM SILEO

SIMON & SCHUSTER

New York   London   Toronto   Sydney   New Delhi

Simon & Schuster
1230 Avenue of the Americas
New York, NY 10020

First Simon & Schuster hardcover edition November 2017

SIMON & SCHUSTER and colophon are registered trademarks
of Simon & Schuster, Inc.

For information about special discounts for bulk purchases,
please contact Simon & Schuster Special Sales at 1-866-506-1949
or business@simonandschuster.com.

The Simon & Schuster Speakers Bureau can bring authors to
your live event. For more information or to book an event contact
the Simon & Schuster Speakers Bureau at 1-866-248-3049 or visit
our website at www.simonspeakers.com.

Interior design by Lewelin Polanco

Manufactured in the United States of America

10 9 8 7 6 5 4 3 2 1

Library of Congress Cataloging-in-Publication Data is available.

ISBN 978-1-5011-6588-7
ISBN 978-1-5011-6589-4 (ebook)

To US Army Command Sergeant Major Kevin Griffin, US Army Major Tom Kennedy, US Air Force Major David Gray, USAID Foreign Service Officer Ragaei Abdelfattah, and your families. I will never forget you, nor will the grateful nation for which you made the ultimate sacrifice.

—FLO GROBERG

To my grandparents, Canio and Hedy Sileo and Clarence and Betty Luther. Your sacrifices during World War II helped pave the way for future generations of American heroes.

—TOM SILEO

CONTENTS

8 SECONDS OF COURAGE

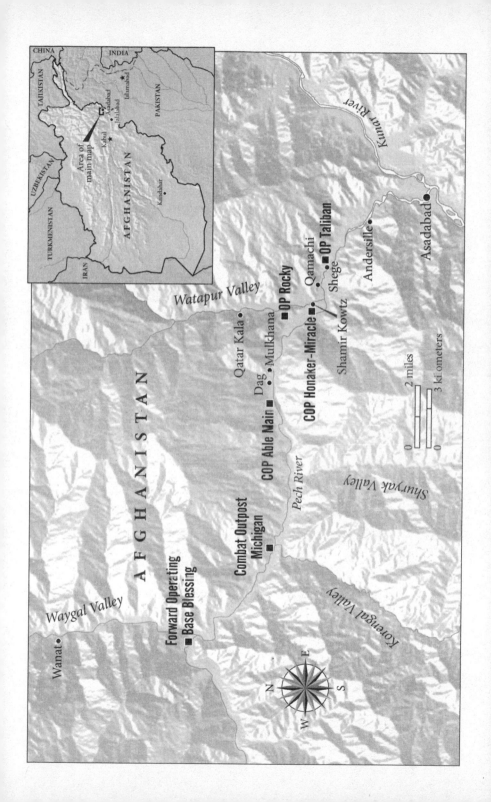

1 TOY SOLDIERS

I had never thought about quitting anything until the United States Army Ranger School's "Mountain Phase" in the rugged hills of Dahlonega, Georgia. By the fortieth day of Ranger School in October 2009, my lifelong dislike of hiking had turned into pure hatred.

I had to get through only twenty-one more days to earn the Army's coveted Ranger tab, but after six weeks of constant fatigue, I was just about finished. Like most of my fellow soldiers, I had lost around twenty pounds due to strictly imposed food limits, and hadn't slept more than four hours a night since Ranger School began. For me, those challenges were nothing compared to hiking up and down Ranger Camp Frank D. Merrill's ruthless cliffs. The mountains of North Georgia were my kryptonite.

On the fortieth night, my thirteen-man squad and I were on what we called a "death march," which started in the dead of night and wouldn't end until we reached a mock objective at 0500. Thankfully it was neither too hot nor cold in early October, but an unrelenting rainstorm made my wet, muddy boots feel as if they were filled with concrete. Even with my night optical devices (NODs), I could barely see the tree branches that were constantly snapping into my face. Bugs were all over my body and inside my dry, thirsty mouth.

I knew that these hardships were designed to prepare us for many months of combat in the mountains of Afghanistan, where I would likely deploy after Ranger School. But I was physically and mentally drained, with a stomach buckling in on itself. All I could think about was how much this sucked. My deteriorating legs and body language made it even more obvious that I was struggling.

"What's wrong?" another Ranger candidate, Staff Sergeant Erick Gallardo, said.

"Hell," I said while gasping for air. "I can't take this shit anymore."

"What do you mean?" he said. "Are you falling asleep?"

Guys passing out during simulated missions, even while standing up or marching, was commonplace. For me, though, it was about more than sleep deprivation. I felt like forty straight days of Ranger School's nonstop chaos had finally broken me.

"I'm smoked, man," I told Gallardo. "I think I'm done."

After a pause, Gallardo, who had narrowly survived a bullet striking his helmet in eastern Afghanistan's infamous Korengal Valley, made me an offer.

"If you quit right now, I'll quit with you," he said.

Gallardo had received a Silver Star for his heroic actions as the leader of a 173rd Airborne Brigade Combat Team squad that included Army Staff Sergeant Salvatore Giunta (who would later receive the Medal of Honor). Gallardo had been through a lot worse than the mountains of North Georgia. Even though he had nearly been killed in Afghanistan, Gallardo wanted to return to the battlefield as a platoon sergeant, which required earning the Ranger tab.

If I quit, it wouldn't just be a huge setback to my military career; it would mess up Gallardo's future, too.

"Get through this damn patrol and sleep on it," he continued. "If you feel the same way in the morning, we'll quit tomorrow."

Gallardo gave me the second wind I needed, and out of habit my mind snapped back to a concept that had been drilled into my head since the beginning of Ranger School: leave no man behind. After getting through nearly six hellish weeks, why should I give up and take another soldier down with me? Quitting was contrary to everything I stood for.

The next day, the sun came out for the first time in a long while.

"Are we quitting today?" Gallardo inquired as we wolfed down our MREs (Meals, Ready to Eat).

"Negative," I said.

But the next night, I reached a second breaking point during another eleven-hour death march. That made our total time awake twenty-three hours. With one hour to go, I was frantically searching for a piece of lost gear, and soon realized I was hallucinating from exhaustion.

My Ranger buddy had hurt his ankle a few meters earlier, which prompted me to grab his tripod and add it to the pile of gear that was already on my back. I was carrying over one hundred pounds, in addition to my M240 machine gun. The enormous weight, combined with the pitch-black darkness and brutal terrain, caused me to trip and fall into the mud—fifteen separate times.

Each time I fell, I worried that I would accidentally discharge my weapon, which would have resulted in my immediate dismissal from Ranger School. Each time I got up, it became harder and harder to lift the hundred-pound weight on my back.

After the fifteenth fall, my backpack—or "ruck" as we say in the military—felt lighter. Either my hallucinations were worsening, I thought, or a piece of gear was missing.

That's when I realized that the tripod had disappeared somewhere in the darkness, along with—in all likelihood—my chances of graduating from Ranger School. Like an accidental gun discharge, losing your Army equipment was a serious offense, and the Ranger Instructors (RIs) had zero sympathy for this scenario.

For the sixteenth time, I fell down, this time out of complete mental obliteration rather than physical fatigue. The thought of fifteen months of hard work—from US Army Basic Training, Officer Candidate School, and the Basic Officer Leadership Course to Infantry School, Airborne School, and now Ranger School—ending in failure was devastating. Many of my peers did not think highly of an infantry officer without a Ranger tab. I had chosen to undergo what was probably the Army's toughest training regimen because I wanted to lead soldiers in combat, but in that moment my path to war was muddier than the ground I was lying on.

When I looked up, I could barely make out a familiar face staring down at me.

"Get up, Groberg," Gallardo said. "We've got too much fun left; you don't want to miss it!"

Ranger School challenges everything about a human being. It challenges your mind, your body, your emotions, your leadership, your decision making, and most important, your attitude. As Gallardo demonstrated while sensing my struggles, there was also nowhere to hide. From the RIs to your peers, everybody was watching.

Eventually, I found my way to my feet and looked at Gallardo. It's rare to face a career decision that can clearly change the trajectory of your life, but for me this was one of those defining moments. While thinking about what to do for a few seconds, I forgot where I was.

"You are about to embark upon the Great Crusade, toward which we have striven these many months," I said in French. "The eyes of the world are upon you.

"Your task will not be an easy one," I continued. "Your enemy is well trained, well equipped and battle hardened. He will fight savagely."

Seconds later, I moved an army of little green plastic soldiers into formation. In a few moments, they would unleash a furious assault on a nearly identical army of gray plastic men.

"I have full confidence in your courage, devotion to duty and skill in battle," I said. "We will accept nothing less than full victory. Good luck!"

I was quoting General Dwight D. Eisenhower's famous letter to US troops before the Allied liberation of France, where I was born. As a nine-year-old boy, I was busy reenacting World War II, which I had been obsessed with since learning to read. From a young age, playing with toy soldiers inside my room in the Paris suburb of Achères had been my favorite activity.

As my plastic army assaulted Normandy's heavily fortified shores, which were actually pillows, my voice would frequently change as I pretended to belt out commands from the respective green and gray army commanders.

"ATTACK," I shouted.

Before long, though, D-Day was interrupted.

"Flo?" my mother, Klara Groberg, said. "Stop talking to yourself!"

"I'm not talking to myself," I said assertively. "It's the soldiers!"

Eventually, my mom became so concerned that my pretend violence was influencing my behavior at school that she took me to a doctor. Fortunately, the family physician told her that young boys playing war was nothing to be concerned about.

It was common culture in France to aspire to one day put on a uniform and become a soldier. In my mind, fighting the bad guys always made sense, and for as long as I could remember, I was fascinated by the concept of defeating an enemy, and in particular moving troops into position for battle. To be honest, I understood—even at a young age—how that could be concerning to a mother.

Despite common dreams, my path to the US Army was different from that of most soldiers, mainly because I was born in France. As American kids grew up in the Reagan, Bush, and Clinton years, my character was primarily molded in the relatively poor suburbs of Paris between 1983 and 1994. I also lived in Spain for a short time and frequently visited Algeria, where my mother was born and raised before she moved to France and eventually met my father, Larry Groberg.

My mom first took me to Algeria when I was three months old. I was the grandparents' first grandchild (albeit my mom has eleven siblings), and I had nearly died in the hospital after being born three months premature. Therefore, my mom bringing me to North Africa, where she had grown up during the brutal Algerian War in the 1950s, was a monumental moment for my family.

My uncle, Abd Alillah Lahreche (who went by Abdou), was ecstatic upon my early arrival. To this day, my mom, the eldest sibling, can vividly recall handing me over to her younger brother.

"I am your Uncle Abdou," he said in Arabic while staring straight into my little eyes. "You are my Flo."

Even though he had no experience caring for children, let alone babies when he was only eighteen years old, Uncle Abdou treated me as if I were his own son. On that very first day, he held me on his chest for several hours while I took a nice, long nap.

Quickly, Uncle Abdou became that one person that all young children cling to. He took his role as a guardian as seriously as his name, which means "servant of God" in Arabic.

"You are my Flo," he repeated. "I won't let anything happen to you."

Starting in my preschool years, I would regularly visit my grandparents, aunts, and uncles in Algeria, but my connection to Uncle Abdou became so strong that even when my mom and I would make unannounced visits, my uncle had already told other family members about my impending arrival. We always joked that Uncle Abdou knew when I was coming to visit because of the unwavering bond we shared.

Abdou also made it a priority to visit my family in France during a week-long gap between the start of French and Algerian schools. On the day of his arrival, I would sit atop the steps leading to my family's apartment and wait for my idol. Regardless of whether my wait lasted minutes or hours, I was always nervous that he wouldn't appear. I wouldn't eat, drink, or play with my toy soldiers until I saw him open the front door.

After Uncle Abdou would arrive and give me a hug and kiss on the forehead, without fail he would say "You are my Flo" . . . every single time.

"You are my Abdou," I would respond.

Over dinners that were more like feasts, I overheard stories about the horrors of the war in Algeria. Uncle Abdou didn't have a military background, but he still managed to impart crucial values about good and evil to me throughout those dinners. My uncle also taught me that liberty wasn't granted to all.

"Freedom has to be earned," Uncle Abdou said. "Sometimes, you have to fight for it."

My uncle was a devout Muslim. My mom grew up in the same household and was brought up the same way, but I was not raised Muslim. Instead I followed my father's Lutheran faith.

Despite my Christian upbringing, my parents still encouraged me to attend the mosque with Uncle Abdou, where I would watch him carry out Islam's most sacred traditions. It took only one visit for me to develop enormous respect for my uncle's authentic commitment to his faith.

By the time my family moved across the Atlantic to the Chicago suburb of Palatine, Illinois, when I was twelve, a radical Islamist organization known as GIA—or Groupe Islamique Armé in

French—was causing mass chaos as it terrorized innocent Algerian men, women, and children beginning in 1992.

As I heard about what was happening in Algeria while I was struggling to adapt in an unfamiliar country, I also learned that my uncle's lesson about freedom was not empty rhetoric. After watching in horror as fellow Algerians were murdered, raped, and dismembered, Uncle Abdou swore an oath to fight terrorism as a soldier in the Algerian army.

My mom didn't tell me until later, but when he joined the military, my uncle told her that he wasn't afraid of dying for his country. He was, however, deeply fearful of being tortured by the ruthless GIA terrorists, whose crimes against humanity were similar to the present-day barbarism of the Islamic State, or ISIS.

"I want to die the right way," Uncle Abdou told my mom.

Even though I was still a boy, my uncle's courage was deeply inspirational. Not only was Uncle Abdou like a big brother; he had fulfilled my personal dream of becoming a soldier.

Shortly after my twelfth birthday, we moved from the Chicago area to the Washington, D.C., suburb of Bethesda, Maryland. My English was getting better, but still needed a lot of work. Just as in Illinois, the combination of ESL (English as a Second Language) classes and competitive sports probably did the most to speed my adaptation. Still, America was new and different. Adjusting was not easy.

It was an exciting, bustling time to be an American teenager as the economy boomed and the country prepared to host the 1996 Summer Olympics in Atlanta, but when you don't know much English, you feel like an outsider. Learning a new language was the biggest challenge of my youth, so I attacked it with the same vigor as in those mock D-Day invasions. While we spoke French inside our new home in Maryland, my mom and dad had a strict rule: as soon as we stepped out the front door, we spoke only English.

I realized my English had improved a great deal when I began to watch and understand classic war movies in English, without subtitles. I don't suppose most people think of the early *Rambo* films and *Platoon* being tools for teaching a language, but that's exactly what those movies did for me.

I tried to keep in touch with Uncle Abdou, but it became difficult with him fighting the GIA on Algeria's front lines. When we had last spoken a few months earlier, on Christmas Eve, he had told me that while war is terrible and scary, he knew that fighting evil was the right thing to do. Even though I was an easily distracted teenager who didn't fully understand how much danger my uncle was facing, he was a constant source of inspiration.

As Uncle Abdou and the Algerian army fought halfway around the world in February 1996, I went on a school trip to a Smithsonian museum with my classmates. When I returned to Bethesda, I noticed that my mom wasn't there, which was very unusual for our regular routine. I asked my dad where she was, and he said that I would be able to talk to her soon. I believed my father, but also sensed trepidation in his voice.

Before I knew it, my dad and I were sitting in our living room.

What is going on? Am I in trouble? Where is Mom?

"Florent, I know that this is going to be hard for you to hear," my father began.

Did something happen to my mother?

"Your mom is in Algeria," my dad said. "She is there for a funeral."

What? My head started spinning.

"It's your Uncle Abdou," my father said. "He's been killed."

My vision narrowed until it became a pinhole of light. I suddenly had no control over my body or my emotions.

A few seconds later, I fainted and hit the floor. *This can't be happening.*

What I still didn't know was that early that morning, my mom had had to be sedated prior to her painful flight to Algeria. The death of her brother had destroyed her, much as it was now destroying me.

I was told that Uncle Abdou's murder came at the hands of the GIA. While my father did his best to comfort me, the details of Uncle Abdou's death were gruesome and inhumane. As a twelve-year-old, I learned my uncle wasn't just killed in battle: he was beheaded, dismembered, and his body parts shipped back to my extended family in a box.

As my mother would tell me upon returning from Algeria, the only saving grace was that Uncle Abdou had been shot through the heart. That was my mom's only comfort after her brother had expressed his fear of being tortured. According to Abdou's religion, he was in a better place now. In Islam, life on earth is only preparation for the eternal life to come. The Muslim faith dictates that Allah will balance the good deeds a person has done in his or her life against the bad deeds. If the good outweighs the bad, the person will go to paradise: a place of joy and bliss.

I didn't go to school for an entire week after being told about Uncle Abdou's death because I was so upset. With my mom still in Algeria, my dad stayed home from work because he was worried about me. He had never seen his only son experience these kinds of emotions, and frankly, I didn't know how to handle them. Never in my life had I felt that kind of piercing grief and unbridled rage. I didn't want to sit around mourning my uncle. I wanted to find his killers and bring them to justice.

It's hard to remember much else from that week other than one moment. As soon as I walked in my room and wiped away the tears, I went straight to my drawer and pulled out those two plastic bags full of green and gray soldiers. Bags in tow, I walked downstairs, past my dad.

"Flo, where are you going?" he asked as I walked out the back door. Defiantly, I ignored him. A few moments later, I had started burning my toy soldiers in a makeshift fire pit.

As the green and gray plastic melted, I had a paradigm shift in the way I thought about religion. I remember thinking, *How can people use religion to justify murder, rape, and dismemberment?* I did not associate myself with a religion after that day because too many used it as fuel for violence, but I continued to believe in God.

War was no longer a game. From that night forward, I was finished with toy soldiers.

Staring through the darkness up at Staff Sergeant Gallardo, I knew it was time to decide whether I should quit Ranger School and head back to my regular Army unit, or keep moving forward. Mountain Phase had absolutely kicked my ass, but if I decided to leave, this friend and Afghanistan war veteran was leaving North Georgia with me.

Still, I couldn't find that damn tripod that had fallen off my ruck, which would almost certainly result in me getting kicked out of Ranger School anyway.

"Are we quitting?" Gallardo asks.

Before I could answer, another soldier interrupted.

"Hey bro, do you know why you keep falling?" he said. "The tripod is dangling from your ruck, so you're dragging it through the mud."

This revelation was so obvious it was almost comical. It sent waves of energy through my tired body and mind. I hadn't lost the tripod after all.

Before thanking our observant fellow soldier, I answered Gallardo.

"Negative," I said. "Let's keep pushing."

Covered in dark brown mud and finishing the death march in the black of night, I was suddenly the happiest soldier in the world. It was 0400, so if I could make it through the next hour, I knew that I would conquer the last three weeks of Ranger School, too.

"We can do this," I said to the guy walking next to me.

"Who are you talking to, Groberg?" a squad member walking behind me asked.

"Mickey Mouse," I replied.

Honest to God, the figure to my left looked exactly like a costumed Mickey Mouse you would see mobbed by adoring children at Disney World. When I reached out, I could even touch his white, puffy hand.

"Bro, you're hallucinating," another soldier said.

I no longer cared. The death march was almost over, and as I described Mickey Mouse's big, black ears, my Ranger School brothers shared a hearty laugh at my expense. We were all relieved to experience that brief moment of humor.

When my teammates, Mickey, and I reached our objective, we collapsed like a house of cards. The RIs told us that the next day would start in exactly twenty-five minutes, which left us with two choices: eat our MREs or take a quick nap.

During my time at Ranger School, I learned the difference between what we called a "Hungry Ranger" and a "Sleepy Ranger." Myself, I tended to be a Hungry Ranger, so the choice was easy: I always picked eating over sleeping. Mickey Mouse slowly faded as desperately needed food and water began to stabilize my system.

When the hallucinations finally subsided, I pulled a piece of unread mail out of my pocket.

Inside the envelope was a letter from my dad, which was scribbled onto bar napkins. In it, he described drinking a beer and eating a steak while watching the Chicago Bears, which had been our favorite NFL team since we first moved to Illinois from France.

To be honest, the contents of his letter kind of pissed me off, as I would have given anything to wash a New York strip down with a cold one. I would remind him about that letter for years to come. Still, my dad had taken the time to write me, which meant a lot. As I enjoyed those twenty-five minutes of downtime, I allowed myself to mentally escape Ranger School.

I was a freshman at the University of North Carolina–Wilmington on September 11, 2001. Like anyone old enough to remember, I was rocked by the first images of the World Trade Center's burning North Tower, which I saw on my dorm's shared television. As black smoke billowed up into the skies above lower Manhattan and the Statue of Liberty, which had been a gift from the country where I was born, I suddenly felt the same sense of rage I experienced on the night my uncle was murdered.

Instead of retreating to my room to find something to burn, I picked up the phone and called home.

"Mom, they did it again," I said as soon as she answered. I was thinking of Uncle Abdou.

"Flo?" she said with the same concerned voice I heard whenever she was worried about me. "Are you all right?"

"They're knocking down the World Trade Center in New York," I said in French. "Turn on the TV."

When she started watching, the World Trade Center was still standing, and the South Tower hadn't yet been struck. Even though it was impossible to conclude that 9/11 was a terrorist event from the very beginning, I just *knew*. Perhaps the awful experience of losing an uncle to the same evil ideology gave me the preconceived notion. For whatever reason, I had no doubt that America was being attacked.

I heard my mom drop to the floor in anguish when the second

plane hit. Five short years after she had been in Algeria for Uncle Abdou's funeral and witnessed the devastation to her homeland as a result of the GIA, like-minded terrorists were attacking her new country just a few hundred miles from where she lived. I, too, began to panic when American Airlines Flight 77 crashed into the Pentagon.

Of course, Osama bin Laden and his psychotic followers were not the same terrorists who had dismembered my uncle in Algeria, but al Qaeda and the GIA were one and the same to me.

"Mom, put Dad on the phone," I asked.

After my father picked up the phone, I told him that I was going to quit college and enlist in the United States Army as a Ranger. The terrorists had done this to my family in 1996 and now to my adopted country. There was no way that I was going to stand on the sidelines and not be a part of the solution.

My father silently listened to me vent about my frustration and anger. Once I was done, he told me that he was angry as well, but it was in these specific moments that I really had to take a step back and not make a decision based on emotion.

He then asked me if I remembered what he made me promise.

Though I couldn't remember, my father made sure to remind me.

"When I gave you the name Groberg, I told you that it came with a specific requirement," he said. "When we start something, we finish it.

"I know that you are angry," he continued. "So are millions of Americans, and guess what? We all should be. But if you decide to quit school to join the military, you will always find a reason to quit anything that you have started."

My dad's advice—delivered on September 11, 2001—was profound.

"You are a man and you can make your own decisions," he said in conclusion. "Remember: the tough decision usually isn't the most popular. But I expect you to make the right one."

My father was correct. He never let me down and always took the time to teach the right lessons. In this case, I might have hated his answer, but I nevertheless understood his perspective.

As soon as I hung up the phone, I heard singing. I realized it was coming from the television, where Republican and Democratic members of Congress—hand in hand on the steps of the United States Capitol—were singing "God Bless America." My throat clenched and my eyes welled.

That night, I went to bed understanding that I wouldn't join the military the following morning, but my future in the military was solidified. I would put on a military uniform sooner rather than later.

Following the attacks of September 11, 2001, I was no longer a guy from France. From that day forward, I was an American.

After finishing Mountain Phase and then successfully navigating the swamps of Florida, which marked Ranger School's final challenge, I embraced my mom and dad after the US Army Ranger tab was pinned on my shoulder during a ceremony at Fort Benning. I also finally got to sit down and eat! I had never been that hungry in my life, and for about a week, this Hungry Ranger ate every meal as if his life depended on it. I also made my dad take me out on the town for the steak and beer he had joked about in that letter.

Of the three-hundred-plus soldiers in our original Ranger School class, just sixty-nine of us graduated. The fact that I was one of them meant a great deal to my parents, who knew that my path to becoming a soldier started because of Uncle Abdou and was cemented on 9/11. They were also naturally scared for my safety, but seeing me earn the Army Ranger tab made them proud.

Ranger School is a leadership school, but in my opinion it is also a test of character. It wasn't any ordinary camping trip, but a life lesson learned through trial by fire. I learned a lot about myself and my peers during those two trying months.

With the support of my Ranger buddies, I had made it through the hardest challenge of my life. Getting to celebrate the achievement with my family and brothers-in-arms like Staff Sergeant Gallardo was a privilege. After so much hunger, exhaustion, and self-doubt, I knew that those sixty-one days of hell had made me a better soldier, and a better person. To this day, I live by the US Army Ranger Creed.

Recognizing that I volunteered as a Ranger, fully knowing the hazards of my chosen profession, I will always endeavor to uphold the prestige, honor, and high esprit de corps of the Rangers.

Acknowledging the fact that a Ranger is a more elite soldier who arrives at the cutting edge of battle by land, sea, or air, I accept the fact that as a Ranger my country expects me to move further, faster and fight harder than any other soldier.

Never shall I fail my comrades. I will always keep myself mentally alert, physically strong and morally straight and I will shoulder more than my share of the task whatever it may be, one-hundred-percent and then some.

Gallantly will I show the world that I am a specially selected and well-trained soldier. My courtesy to superior officers, neatness of dress and care of equipment shall set the example for others to follow.

Energetically will I meet the enemies of my country. I shall defeat them on the field of battle for I am better trained and will fight with all my might. Surrender is not a Ranger word. I will never leave a fallen comrade to fall into the hands of the enemy and under no circumstances will I ever embarrass my country.

Readily will I display the intestinal fortitude required to fight on to the Ranger objective and complete the mission though I be the lone survivor.

Rangers lead the way!

Just six weeks after graduating Ranger School, I was in Afghanistan.

2 SHUT UP AND LISTEN

Even through the war-torn night sky, I could tell that eastern Afghanistan's jagged, soaring cliffs would be a lot tougher than the mountains of North Georgia.

I had already been in Afghanistan for three days after stops in Germany, Romania, and Kyrgyzstan, but it wasn't until our helicopter landed at Forward Operating Base (FOB) Blessing that I felt like I was really at war. It was surreal to finally have approached the moment that I waited for my entire life. I kept Uncle Abdou in the forefront of my mind a lot during those first few weeks on the ground.

Until you are in a combat situation, it is impossible to know how you will react. After seventeen months of intense training, there I was making a nighttime landing in Afghanistan's treacherous Pech River Valley, which is near the country's border with Pakistan. Hundreds of American soldiers had already been killed and wounded in this valley of death, and in a matter of minutes my journey would start with a bang.

Despite everything that the Army does to prepare a second lieutenant like me for his or her first night at war, even the most competent military leaders question whether they're truly ready to take command of a platoon in battle. I learned this the hard way as our Chinook landed at FOB Blessing with a literal and proverbial thud.

"Go, go, go!" several soldiers on the ground shouted at us.

Given that we were landing on an American base, I was a surprised that we had to hurry off the helicopter, but as the highest-ranking officer, I was responsible for every soldier on board.

"Haul ass," I shouted at my fellow passengers. "Let's go."

Whipping dirt filled my eyes as I exited the helicopter. More yelling from soldiers on the ground, along with the deafening sounds of the chopper's revolving blades had me hearing white noise. I knew that the soldiers wanted us to hustle, but still didn't fully understand the situation's urgency.

That changed when the soldiers on board and I arrived next to a guard tower and were instructed to crouch down.

"Take cover under the guard tower, sir," a senior Army noncommissioned officer (NCO) said. "Right here and right now, we are going to make a few things clear."

Shit. I screwed up already?

"When I tell you to giddy up, Lieutenant, *that means you move your ass,*" he shouted directly into my already ringing ears. "Y'all were taking rocket-propelled grenades!"

To my complete shock and embarrassment, the soldiers I had been responsible for were under attack—and I didn't even know it. The pitch-black darkness combined with the helicopter noise made it almost impossible to comprehend that we were taking fire, but that was no excuse. In five minutes, I learned my first lesson from "The Stan," a common military nickname for Afghanistan.

"Roger," I said as firmly as I could manage under such circumstances. I had to meet with the battalion commander the next morning, and knew that I would almost certainly face tough questions about my failure to lead.

My soldiers, whom I had never met, had spent 2009's violent

summer fighting season squaring off with insurgents and terrorists while I was busy hallucinating on death marches through the North Georgia mountains. Even though finishing Ranger School was the reason I was showing up mid-deployment, it didn't change the fact that I was as green as a platoon leader could be, and would therefore be viewed with skepticism by the men I was supposed to lead.

As I tried to sleep during that first night at FOB Blessing, named in honor of fallen Army Sergeant Jay Blessing, who made the ultimate sacrifice six years earlier in the valley, I was restless. My mind was racing through what had just happened and what I could have done differently.

Meanwhile, inside our transient barracks, nineteen soldiers were sleeping in cots that were just inches from mine. Hours earlier, we could have all been killed by the Taliban, and yet these young men were sleeping like babies. Unbeknownst to me at the time, this would become a normal feeling as an officer in charge of troops.

While chatting with some of the officers around the compound the following morning, I did everything I could to gather some tips that would help me as I took over my future platoon. I knew that in about ten days, I would travel about forty-five minutes southeast in a convoy headed to Combat Outpost (COP) Honaker-Miracle, which was closer to the Pakistani border than FOB Blessing. COPs are generally smaller than FOBs, which serve as logistical hubs.

At COP Honaker-Miracle, I would assume responsibility for one of two Army platoons on the COP: 4th Platoon, Dagger Company. As platoon leader, I would be charged with the difficult task of leading twenty-four soldiers through the Taliban- and al Qaeda-infested valley, where our mission would be relatively straightforward: kill the bad guys and protect seven villages, all while somehow winning the hearts and minds of the local Afghan population.

I had limited time to get acclimated to the environment and the unit. Luckily, a lieutenant colonel named Pearl had tasked me with leading a patrol for him during my fourth day at the FOB. On the mission, we would walk approximately two miles from Blessing toward one of the observational posts overlooking the valley. I remember thinking that I didn't have much room to screw up considering the highest-ranking officer in my area of operations (AO) was joining us.

The first mile took us north of the base, following a road leading to a mountain pass. From there, it was one mile straight up the mountain. Though the rigorous training of Ranger School had prepared me for this walk, this wasn't the case for a private named Campbell, who had deployed with me from Fort Carson. Halfway up the mountain, PVT Campbell decided that he had had enough, and took a seat.

"Campbell, what in the hell are you doing?" I yelled at him.

"Sorry, sir," he responded through short breaths. "I'm just exhausted."

"Shit man . . . get up—the battalion commander is going to have both of our asses," I screamed.

Just then, I heard the lieutenant colonel's voice.

"GROBERG!" LTC Pearl yelled as he moved up closer to Campbell. "Why do we have a break in contact?"

"Sorry, sir," I immediately responded. "Private Campbell rolled his ankle and we are stabilizing it."

It was a white lie. I was ready to take the heat for Campbell because this was my patrol. To be honest, I could sympathize with him as well.

Pearl didn't need to worry about a private going down due to exhaustion, so I grabbed Campbell by the arm and brought him to his feet.

"Don't quit on me and I won't quit on you, got it?" I said while reminding myself of what another soldier had done for me during Ranger School. "We can rest at the top."

"Roger, sir," Campbell responded.

When we eventually made it to the top of the mountain, the view was breathtaking. I took off my helmet and passed a water bottle to Campbell, who thanked me for covering for him.

This day was the first day in Afghanistan that I felt like I had accomplished something. That night was also the first time I joined the orchestra of nineteen snoring infantrymen.

Unfortunately, my first night of shut-eye wasn't quite as relaxing as I expected. After drifting off to sleep, I started dreaming of the last time I was unprepared and lacked confidence: my incredibly awkward freshman year of high school.

"O Romeo, Romeo!" the prettiest girl at Walter Johnson High School in Bethesda, Maryland, said while looking squarely into my young, very wide eyes. "Wherefore art thou Romeo?"

After my very lovely counterpart effortlessly finished her lines during a dress rehearsal of *Romeo and Juliet*, it was my turn.

"Shall I . . . hear more," I stammered in broken English. "Or shall I spoke—I mean speak—at this?"

As the disastrous rehearsal continued, I turned bright red and beads of sweat popped up on my forehead. Some of my classmates were openly snickering at my poor command of the English language, which I had been studying for quite a few years by that point. Yet with my nerves surfacing, I sounded like a brand-new immigrant.

To make matters worse, this embarrassing scene was unfolding in front of my real-life Juliet. I had wanted to ask this girl out since the first day of high school.

"I take she—thee—at thy world—word," I said. "Call me butt— I mean call me but love—damn it, and I'll be new baptized."

By now, even my Juliet was laughing at me. My heart sank as I realized that my semester-long dream of taking her on a date was officially over.

"Henceforth, I will never be Romeo," I recited with my shoulders slumped. Fittingly, it was just about the only line I got right.

Clearly, I wasn't ready for Shakespeare. At home that evening, I told my parents, in French, about what had happened at school earlier in the day. While my mom was sympathetic, my dad took a different approach.

"Stop whining and study harder," he said.

"But it's impossible, Dad," I said. "English is nothing like French."

"Who the hell told you that life was easy?" he shot back.

Suddenly, my dad broke his own rule and started speaking English inside the house instead of French.

"That school has great teachers," he said. "Stay after school and ask one of them to help you with your English."

"Okay, Dad," I said in French. "Whatever."

"Tell me that in English," he said.

After I did just that, my dad stared me down. While the *Romeo and Juliet* debacle was a bitter pill to swallow, especially for a teenager, I made a conscious choice to use the embarrassing episode as motivation to improve my English. Instead of starting fights with the male classmates who taunted me, I took my dad's advice and stayed after school for extra tutoring.

By the year 2000, I was learning the language faster than I ever thought possible. My hard work finally paid off during my junior year, when I was enrolled in Honors English and sat next to many of the same kids who had laughed in my face two years earlier.

Take that, Juliet.

On December 21, 2009, I arrived at COP Honaker-Miracle, where both American and Afghan soldiers were stationed. The makeshift mountain base was named after two fallen US Army heroes: Specialist Christopher Honaker and Private First Class Joseph Miracle, who were among thirty-nine soldiers killed during the 173rd Brigade Combat Team's 2007-to-2008 deployment to Pech River Valley. This was also where my Ranger School mentor, SSG Gallardo, earned his Silver Star.

When I arrived at the COP, the first thing I did was wait on line to call my dad. There were only four computers and one phone for the ninety soldiers stationed there, which we also shared with the Afghan National Army (ANA). Still, getting to speak to my dad was always well worth the wait.

"I don't know how I'm going to do it, Dad," I said. "These guys have all been here fighting for months already, and I don't know anything. I don't feel prepared."

"Of course you're not prepared," my father said. "Nobody is ever prepared for war."

"Yeah, but I'm responsible for their lives," I said. "I don't care what happens to me—I care about them."

"Well I care a lot about what happens to you," my dad said, his voice beginning to rise.

"Ask your most senior NCO for support," my father said. "Trust me; he will be glad to hear that from you."

A lot of fathers might have told their sons to do whatever they could to *avoid* combat. My dad, on the other hand, knew how much leading a platoon in battle meant to me, especially with my family history in mind. The fact that he set aside his fears for my safety and helped me become a better soldier gave me a huge confidence boost at a time when I needed it most.

Later that day, I went to see Sergeant First Class Korey Staley, a tough, seasoned soldier who—along with the outgoing platoon leader—had successfully helped lead Dagger Company through the Pech River Valley's chaotic summer fighting season.

"I know what you and your men just went through," I told SFC Staley. "I also know that I'm a rookie and your guys probably aren't too excited about another amateur.

"But I stand in front of you asking for your support and guidance," I continued. "I am setting my rank, my pride, and my ego aside to tell you that to be the most effective platoon leader, I will need you to be my mentor. I only care about taking care of our men and accomplishing the mission."

After I finished my speech, Staley told me—in blunt terms—what I needed to do.

"For the next seven days, I think you should shut up and listen, sir," he said.

It was crucial, Staley explained, for me to spend the next week "outside the wire," or outside our base's relatively friendly confines, so that I could observe my new platoon in action. Under no circumstances—whether it was an IED (improvised explosive device) attack or a Taliban fighter shooting at us—was I to do anything other than watch and learn.

Staley wanted me to absorb how the platoon reacted to contact once engaged by the enemy. He also wanted me to observe how soldiers on the ground communicated with each other, how they coordinated mortar fire back with the closest US base, and how information was relayed to helicopters or airplanes to support us. Staley also wanted me to study all seven villages and their elders, while simultaneously learning all that I could about key US battles with the Taliban in the Pech River Valley.

Most important, Staley wanted me to talk to each of the young soldiers whose lives would soon be in my hands.

"Find out if they're married or have kids," he said. "But remember—don't get too close to them, because by this time next week you're going to be their boss."

I would technically be Staley's boss, too, and that's why I especially appreciated his helpful advice.

Presumably, I would spend the next seven days under enemy fire without the ability to shoot back. While Staley's method of showing me the ropes may have given new meaning to the expression "trial by fire," he was clearly taking this unconventional route for an important reason.

"Give me a week, and I'll have you and the platoon ready," my new battlefield mentor said.

It took only two days outside the wire to put Staley's theory—and my intestinal fortitude—to the test. We were driving in a Humvee near a rugged, cliff-surrounded village called Tantil when I first heard an unfamiliar sound: a cannonade noise that sounded far too close.

"Man, every time we hit a pothole, the back doors slam," my driver, Sergeant Mauldin, said. "It makes it sound like we hit an RPG." (A rocket-propelled grenade.)

Boom!

"Um, never mind," SGT Mauldin said. "We *are* getting hit by RPGs!"

All of my training and instincts as a military officer told me to start ordering soldiers around so that we could maneuver and eliminate the threat. Yet as my mouth started to open, I remembered Staley's advice: shut up and listen, even while under attack. So I did exactly that, and even took out my camera to record the firefight. It was surprising to me at the time that during no part of this enemy engagement did I get scared. Instead, I was simply in awe of the fact that other human beings were actively trying to kill us.

There was a wire-guided missile on top of our vehicle manned by a private named Cortez, and in a matter of seconds he had it aimed squarely at a Taliban fighter. Thanks to modern technology, through a command viewer screen I could watch as the missile slammed into what appeared to be the insurgent's stomach. Cortez killed the man's Taliban partner as well, which resulted in a bunch of shouting and high-fiving inside our vehicle.

Even though I played no role in making it happen, that patrol marked the first time I had really seen the reality of combat. At the same time, it made me feel good that I was surrounded by such brave, confident soldiers who could perform with such brilliance under pressure.

We got into a few more firefights over the next five days. It was during that key period that I first realized, even after my training, that modern war was nothing like the *Rambo* movies that I had grown up watching.

In Afghanistan, battles generally started with four or five bad dudes waiting to ambush us with RPGs. Most of the time, they missed in comical fashion while cursing at us over the radio. Despite their primitive tools, the Taliban were incredibly skilled and had the upper hand of knowing their landscape better than we ever could. If they ever got hold of the technological advancements that the US Army used, they would be a super-serious threat.

Our biggest threat—as I was told by Staley, my men, and my commanding officers in mission briefings—was a Taliban commander named Dairon. When Dagger Company was attacked, he was usually the guy calling American soldiers "sons of shits" over the radio in Pashto. While he was widely considered to be a clown who couldn't hold a torch to a US Army general, he was still a clown armed with bullets, bombs, and grenades. Over the next seven months, one of my most important jobs as a platoon leader would be finding a way to take him out.

I kept hearing about Dairon and other threats as my "shut up and listen" week continued. In a stunning coincidence, it also turned out that Saul Thompson, my best friend from the University of Maryland, where I had transferred after a semester at UNC–Wilmington, was leading the COP's other US Army platoon: 3rd Platoon, Chosen Company.

I knew that Saul had previously been assigned to the same battalion and had been deployed since the summer, but I didn't realize that he was at Honaker-Miracle until I got there myself. From that moment on, I knew that no matter what, I would have my best friend with me in combat. *This is going to be fun!*

After a huge hug and a few hearty laughs about the unlikely circumstances of our reunion, I asked Thompson for advice on the massive challenge that I was about to undergo. Like Staley, Thompson told me to get to know my men, while also emphasizing the importance of winning their trust. If I was going to lead my soldiers through life-or-death battles, they had to know that I would always have their backs.

Many of the guys were understandably suspicious of their rookie second lieutenant, and all week they had been testing me by asking ridiculous questions that they knew I couldn't answer without sounding like an idiot.

"Hey L T, how do you zero an M203?" said one soldier, Jones, while referring to his grenade launcher in front of several fellow soldiers.

"Zeroing" is a term commonly used for aligning a rifle's sights in order to precisely aim at a given target. From weapons training, though, I knew that an M203 grenade launcher didn't work that way.

"I don't think you can," I said diplomatically to Jones, not wanting to embarrass him in front of his platoon mates.

"What do you mean you don't think so, L-T?" Jones said. "Are you saying that you don't know your shit?"

Before I could answer, Staley walked in.

"Hey Jones, stop screwing with the new L-T," he said.

Staley then turned in my direction.

"Sir, don't mind them," my mentor said. "It's usually a good sign if they are messing with you."

I understood the game and it didn't bother me at all. In Afghanistan, rank didn't matter nearly as much as experience. If a guy wasn't battle-tested, he'd better have tough skin, so I let it go. Had I been in

Jones's position of putting my life in the hands of someone who had never set foot in a war zone until a few days earlier, I probably would have done the same thing.

My first real test arrived during my second week at Honaker-Miracle, when Staley announced that he was taking a short flight to our base in Jalalabad to complete some administrative tasks.

Despite the progress I had been making over the past few days, I secretly hoped that it would be a quiet, uneventful few nights. Yet as was usually the case in this part of Afghanistan, which we called the "Wild West" even though we were deployed in the easternmost part of the country, the Taliban had other plans.

That night after returning from a routine patrol, I was chatting with Saul in the tactical operations center (TOC), which is like a control room, when one of the sergeants came running in asking for me. The soldier told me that he had a Lieutenant Capasso on the line calling from FOB Blessing.

"Hello, this is Groberg," I answered.

"Look brother, Alpha Company responded to a Troops in Contact [TIC] request in Chapa Dara and they were met by some serious assholes," Capasso told me via satellite phone. "We need you as part of the QRF."

QRF stands for "Quick Reaction Force," which scrambles to support another platoon—including those stationed on other FOBs and COPs—when they get hit.

Capasso would go on to explain that Alpha Company was stuck in the depths of the Pech River Valley. As one of several platoons headed out there to help them, our job was to investigate and then secure a nearby bridge that intelligence officers believed might be booby-trapped with IEDs until Alpha Company crossed it. To reach the bridge, we would have to take four trucks and drive seventy-five minutes through dirt roads along tall, uneven cliffs.

Many of my soldiers thought it was a suicide mission, and I

couldn't disagree with them. Driving through perilous mountains to reach a bridge that was almost certainly booby-trapped wasn't exactly what I had in mind for my first solo mission.

No matter what I may have thought about the thorny task in front of us, it was my job to complete the mission my platoon was given, no matter how difficult or dangerous, and bring everyone home alive. Despite my apprehension and trepidation, that's exactly what I planned on doing.

I rushed back to my room to put on my kit and headphones. Per tradition, I blasted Korn's "Freak on a Leash" to pump myself up before putting on my body armor, knee pads, helmet, and an attached iPro camera lens to record the day's action. Then I ordered my men—who were probably just as nervous about my leadership as they were about what we would encounter on the battlefield—to do the same.

"Let's do this," I told my men as we embarked on a dangerous first journey together into the mountains of eastern Afghanistan.

Tensions were high throughout the bumpy, rocky drive. At any moment, we could have hit an IED or, like the previous mission I had recorded with my phone, gotten pounded by RPGs. I also knew that Dairon and his gang of Taliban were out there somewhere, and that at any moment we could find ourselves in a battle even fiercer than what Alpha Company was enduring.

To make matters worse, the dark, gray Afghan sky suddenly opened, causing massive streams of rainwater to cascade off the cliffs and turn the dirt roads into mud. Nature seemed to be having its way, putting us at an extreme disadvantage and setting up the enemy fighters who were waiting to strike. Needless to say, my first experience leading a platoon in Afghanistan was no walk in the park.

By the time my truck and the three behind us somehow got the bridge in our sights, you could feel Dagger Company's tension about to erupt.

"Sir, I see the bridge, let's stop here," my gunner, Sergeant Richardson, shouted over the radio. "They are probably watching us right now!"

"Everyone scan your sectors," I instructed while trying to stay calm.

While I had just met these guys a few days ago, I already knew from watching them in action that none of them were afraid of a firefight. They were well-trained, experienced soldiers who knew an unnecessary risk when they saw it. Still, I had my orders in hand, and it was my job to figure out a way to follow them.

Just as I was finishing telling my soldiers how we would handle radio traffic as we got closer to the bridge, we heard the panicked voice of one of Dagger Company's sergeants, Wade, who was in another truck.

"*SHIT!*" SGT Wade suddenly screamed on the radio. "*We are going down!*"

"Sir, Wade is in trouble!" my driver said while hitting my arm.

Immediately, I switched communication channels to figure out what was happening. To my surprise, all I could hear was laughter from the team. It turned out that SGT Wade's driver—exhausted from an earlier mission—fell asleep at the wheel and almost drove the second truck off the cliff. Fortunately, he stopped just in time, and everyone was okay.

This was going to be a long night.

As it turned out, when we reached the bridge, we learned that it wasn't booby-trapped. But we would still have to spend several hours guarding the bridge to make sure the Taliban didn't show up to plant IEDs.

The monsoon conditions made it extremely difficult to scan for threats, especially when one of my soldiers spotted a small group of potential enemy fighters on a nearby ridgeline. My biggest fear was that the group was actually made up of American soldiers from the

Alpha Company platoon we were there to support. Before ordering my gunner to fire at them, I needed to confirm our fellow company's location.

After a lengthy process to verify that the men were carrying weapons and not wearing US Army uniforms, my gunner fired, which sent the suspected Taliban insurgents scurrying all over the rain-soaked hills.

We were wet, tired, and exhausted by the time Alpha Company made it to the bridge, but instead of being thanked for our efforts, which included firing at the enemy, I was unexpectedly berated by the battalion commander (BC) for allowing our trucks to park along the mountain face. While I thought I was following normal procedures by staying to the right, the commander was angry that I had forced his vehicle to pass on the edge of one of the area's many steep cliffs.

After some thought, I understood why my four-vehicle convoy blocking most of the narrow mountain road, which made Alpha Company's maneuver home even more hazardous, would piss off the BC.

When we finally got back to the COP, I was scolded yet again, this time for allowing the cagelike wiring designed to shield our vehicles from RPGs to get caught up at Honaker-Miracle's gate, which resulted in damage to one of our trucks. The success of our mission was irrelevant to my commanding officer (CO), who told me that I would have to find and hire Afghan contractors to repair the truck.

The next morning, I had to wake up at 0600 to secure plans for a truck repair, which is not quite as easy as going to your local body shop when you are in the heart of Afghanistan's mountainous Kunar Province.

I would undoubtedly make more mistakes during the many long days of fighting that lay ahead, but even after getting chewed out for the second time, I felt that I might have earned some measure of respect from the platoon for staying calm and completing a tough mission. I still had doubts about whether I could perform all of my duties in Afghanistan, but when I went to sleep that night, I decided to trust in the training I had received.

The following week, I shared our experience with SFC Staley when he got back from Jalalabad.

Staley nodded in acknowledgment, but didn't say much as we stood outside the TOC overlooking the bloody Pech River Valley. He was smoking a cigarette and I was chewing tobacco.

"Fourth Platoon is yours now," Staley said. "Good luck . . . and know that I've got your back."

From that day forward, I knew that twenty-four American lives were in my hands. I was ready, motivated, and understood my role and the importance of my position. I also felt everyone's eyes on me.

For seven days, I had shut up and I listened. For the next seven months, it was time to go hard or go home.

3 PISS AND SHIT

Some of eastern Afghanistan's landscape is the most beautiful in the world. Picture clear blue reservoirs like Thailand, mountain peaks like Sweden, pastures like Ireland, and endless fields of flowers like the Netherlands. With the pervasive threat of death surrounding you, it's often hard to see that beauty, especially amid frigid winter temperatures.

Contrary to the picturesque landscape was our remote combat outpost, where conditions were as bad as it gets. Therefore, my initial impression of Afghanistan was jaded: I thought it was a dirty place.

Inside COP Honaker-Miracle's compounds, the floors were made of concrete but covered by dirt. Clean drinking water was non-existent, which required us to use bottled water when brushing our teeth, and our "reliable" Internet was mostly just the opposite. I was fortunate enough to have my own room, but that's about the only luck I had at the time.

To prevent my lungs from filling with filth, I would roll out a carpet on the floor of my room each night. Still, I would wake up with the taste of dirt on my tongue. I soon learned that it was necessary to cover my bunk with my bivy cover—a woodland camouflage waterproof sleeping bag—during the day.

To top off this lovely experience, I felt like almost everyone in the Pech River Valley hated me. Everything I knew and cherished in my safe Bethesda home was now a distant memory as I lay in a dusty cot.

My small space, which I never took for granted since most soldiers on the COP didn't have the luxury of their own rooms, quickly became my overseas sanctuary. After I returned from my missions each night, my room became the office where I would plan the following day's missions. I even came by a few posters of supermodels, which soon became my classy wall decor.

I remember the third morning in my new room beginning like any other. I woke up at 0600 to my lungs contracting and forcibly coughing. I also needed to piss.

My teeth chattered as I trudged through the hallways, making my way to the makeshift outhouse. The outdoor pissing buckets were covered in thin camouflage canopy netting. While we had Porta Potties at one end of our base, it was convenient to have a makeshift outdoor bathroom right next to our sleeping quarters for wintry conditions, even though it reeked.

"What's up, McPhee?" I said to the Army specialist taking a piss next to me. He was a fuel expert whom I had met a few days earlier.

"Hey, how's it going, L-T?" he said through a yawn.

McPhee was—for lack of a better word—gifted. It wouldn't be long before McPhee was known around COP Honaker-Miracle for his enormous package.

"How in hell did you end up as a fueler in The Stan?" I asked. "Did your porn star application get rejected?"

Just as McPhee and I started to laugh, we were interrupted by a sudden, unmistakable sound of a firecracker in the distance, which was followed by a whizzing sound right past my ear. McPhee, in a natural move to take cover, swung himself around and in doing so, pissed on my leg.

"Oh, shit," he yelled. "They're shooting at us, sir!"

With my private parts in hand, I stood there staring at the wall where the bullet had just struck. A sniper had literally caught two American soldiers with their pants down.

As another round made its way toward me, I ducked and joined McPhee on the ground. We then crawled back to the barracks for cover, where we finally heard the sounds of mortars pounding the mountain where the sniper had set up. A fellow US soldier manning one of the COP's several guard towers had thankfully heard the sniper rifle's popping off and alerted our gunners, who rained hell on the bathroom assailant.

After a minute or two, McPhee and I slowly stood up and dusted ourselves off. We laughed harder in that moment than I would at any point during the rest of my deployment.

"Jesus Christ," I said. "I can't even take a leak in this place, huh?"

"Welcome to The Stan . . . we call this Tuesday morning," McPhee said. "I guess I should have been a porn star after all, huh?"

While laughing about the story at breakfast later that morning, my college friend Saul shared a rumor about the sniper being a militant from Chechnya. That was the first time I heard that the dark caves above the Pech River Valley weren't just filled with Taliban insurgents. There were plenty of al Qaeda terrorists and America-hating foreign fighters up there, too.

"Should be a fun seven months," I said.

"Tell me about it, sir," said a soldier at our table, Private First Class Louis Martinez, who had been fighting alongside the men now under my command for almost five months.

Shortly after my near-death experience in the outhouse, I endured another event that would turn out to be the shittiest night of my young life.

Following an evening visit to Shege, one of the seven Pech River Valley villages my platoon was responsible for protecting, my soldiers and I were sitting down to eat dinner when my translator, a young Afghan National Army soldier we called Shams, came to tell us that he had received a phone call from the elder (similar to a mayor) of Shege.

"Taliban," said Shams, who looked almost exactly like Antonio Banderas. Immediately, I stood up from the table and headed toward the TOC to let our commanding officer know.

Earlier in the week, an Army Psychological Operations (PSYOPS) noncommissioned officer had the brilliant idea of ordering us to go to all seven villages and pass out business cards—yes, *business cards*—with a phone number to reach us if the bad guys entered their village.

The only issue—aside from the already huge problems of bribes and intimidation of villagers by the Taliban—was that every single Afghan I had met in the Pech seemed to care about one thing and one thing only: getting free stuff from the foreigners occupying their land. During the weekly meetings I led at each village, the impoverished Afghans would practically beg me for edible or tradable goods, which were usually more valuable to them than money.

What some in the US Army didn't understand is that almost anyone living in the valley, including a respected elder, wouldn't hesitate to lie through their rarely brushed teeth if they thought it would result in more free stuff. If an Afghan told us he had seen Taliban, perhaps we would regard his village as cooperative, and therefore green-light a construction project they wanted Uncle Sam to pay for.

On a much smaller scale, Afghans overwhelmingly wanted cases of Rip It Energy drinks. For whatever reason, that valley was addicted to sugary sodas. My platoon got more valuable intelligence from locals by handing out Rip Its and Mountain Dews than we ever did by killing a Taliban commander. Ironically, the Rip It Energy drink slogan is "Patriotism . . . if only we could bottle it!"

After I finished talking to the CO, we jumped into our four military vehicles and drove east into the darkness.

"Watch each other's backs," I told my guys over the radio while checking my weapon in my vehicle's passenger's seat.

"Just wait until L-T sees what's really out there," Martinez whispered just loud enough for me to hear over the radio.

It seems my soldiers, already six months into their combat deployment, knew we were walking into a setup. What Martinez was implying by saying "what's really out there" is that there would be nothing at all.

Sure enough, when we arrived after a fifteen-minute ride over the always unpredictable Afghan roads, the village of Shege was dark and quiet, with no Taliban to be found. As I pounded on the elder's door, my platoon was already getting frustrated.

"Just bust the damn door down, L-T," one soldier pleaded.

I didn't disagree with the sentiment, but our rules of engagement (ROE) dictated that we could not enter a home unless accompanied by Afghan soldiers or police. Since we were trying to reach the village before the alleged Taliban fighters left, we didn't have time to round up one of the ANA platoons on the other side of our COP.

"Negative," I told the impatient soldier.

Finally, a woman answered the door, followed by her husband, who was the village elder.

"Taliban," I said to the elder. "You said there were Taliban here."

"No" is the only English word we consistently heard from most of these folks.

"No Taliban, they already left," he told Shams, who then translated for me. Shams was very serious about his job since he could potentially be rewarded with papers to get him out of Afghanistan and possibly to America. I trusted him and his translations.

"Check everything out from here to the ridgeline," I told a soldier who had stayed inside one of our vehicles. "See if any of these guys are running up the mountain."

If our thermal imaging equipment detected a small group trying to disappear into the night, the gunners atop our platoon's vehicles would light them up with missiles and machine gun fire.

After a few minutes of waiting, my radio buzzed.

"Negative, sir," my soldier said. "Nobody's up there."

My platoon had been right all along. The Afghans had indeed lied to us, and one stupid American—me—had taken the bait. I proceeded to berate Shege's elder, even though my translator almost certainly censored the worst of my profanity.

We were on high alert while walking across a small, rickety bridge that led us out of the village. While the most likely scenario was that the elder wanted to trick us into thinking he was cooperative, I also had to consider the worst, which was that the Taliban had paid or forced him into setting up the Americans for an ambush.

I was the last soldier in the platoon crossing the bridge, and even though I couldn't see much, I was walking backward while scanning Shege's outer perimeter for threats. That's when one wooden strip of the flimsy bridge snapped beneath my feet. I plummeted down a few feet into the river below me.

Suddenly, I was surrounded by darkness and a pungent, overwhelming stench. After a few miserable seconds, I realized that I had just plunged into a river of raw sewage.

"Dude, L-T just fell in their shit!" a young sergeant, Troxell, said amongst robust laughter.

"Help me up," I requested between gags. When no one obliged, I realized that my guys weren't exactly eager to jump into a river of shit for some rookie lieutenant.

Pissed off, I pulled myself out of the raw sewage. I ordered my men back into their vehicles.

"Um, sir, you really shouldn't be riding with us," SGT Mauldin said. "You'll stink up the truck for a month."

"With all due respect, Sergeant, you can go f—k yourself," I said while dripping with sarcasm and sewage. "Let's get out of here."

When we got back to the COP, I ran straight toward Honaker-Miracle's fire pit, stripped naked, and proceeded to burn my shit-covered uniform. I then walked into the base's TOC to confront the PSYOPS genius who thought passing out business cards in primitive Afghan villages was a good idea.

In hindsight, it wasn't the best judgment to walk into the TOC completely naked, but as we all know, hindsight is 20/20.

Stunned silence filled the room as I shared the results of our mission with the PSYOPS guy and our first sergeant.

"Just so you know, there were no Taliban out there," I said. "Have a good night."

I then turned my bare ass around and walked out.

Nobody even asked why I was nude, and to my surprise I didn't get into any trouble for my indecent exposure. After the leadership realized that I had fallen into a Great Nile of Shit, they probably decided to let it go.

So that's how my first deployment to Afghanistan began: piss and shit. War is just like the movies, right?

4 THE WILD WEST

My Dagger Company predecessor, Captain Antonio Salinas, described the enormous challenge of leading an infantry platoon through the Pech River Valley in his 2012 book, *Siren's Song.*

> We wear and move in heavy armor. Our weapons and munitions cost thousands of dollars. We can see in the dark, seeing humans in the form of heat signatures many kilometers away under the cover of darkness. We can call for an array of air support, ranging from unmanned aerial vehicles, F-16s, A-10s, to Apaches, and Kiowas. We can drop 2,000-pound laser guided bombs. Our 155's can hit targets, accurately, from miles away using GPS. We can MEDEVAC the wounded and save life. We can air assault supplies and ammo within minutes of a request. We have satellite imagery and can communicate instantly with our comrades utilizing state of the art communication equipment. We are loud, menacing, and, most of all we are ungodly powerful.
>
> Our opponents wear no armor. They wear linen and carry just a few magazines or a few RPG rounds. They have no laser sights on their weapons, any air support, or satellite imagery. They do not have platoons of men waiting to be a Quick

Reaction Force. They can't call for fire on the move, nor see in the dark. They cannot MEDEVAC their wounded. However, they have the heart to persevere. They fight against overwhelming odds and do amazingly well.

While some of my Ranger School buddies had shared stories of spending many long and boring weeks in Afghanistan, Salinas, Staley, and the soldiers under my command had repeatedly warned me that the Pech River Valley was different. My own early experiences—from the bathroom sniper attack to other encounters—also taught me that every minute of every day could be my last.

Upon waking up one winter morning, while dragging my feet to the outhouse and taking an uneventful piss to start my day, I noticed something strange on a calendar that was thumbtacked to one of the COP's big plywood walls.

"Why is there an 'X' on that date in August?" I asked Martinez.

"That was the only day since we've been here that nobody fired a round in our AO sir," he said.

The calendar made me think. *How could we gain more days that were risk-free?* I had an idea. It was probably a bad idea, I thought, but it also might save lives.

That night, I lay in bed reading transcripts of intercepted radio traffic from the previous twenty-four hours. The Taliban wasn't exactly MI6, so we generally knew the frequencies on which they would communicate most often. Unsurprisingly, their conversations were full of chest-thumping rants about allegedly killing ten "kifers" (infidels) during a recent ambush. In fact, zero of my men were injured or killed, but that didn't stop the enemy from spreading the tale to motivate new fighters coming over the border from Pakistan.

"*Inshallah*, we will kill each and every one of those American sons of shits," a Taliban fighter under Dairon's command said during the last recording. *"Allahu Akbar!"*

During the next day's patrol, I had the platoon stop at Observation Post (OP) Taliban, which was built on a steep mountaintop about a mile south of COP Honaker-Miracle and used to be a staging spot for the Afghan mujahideen fighters getting ready to ambush Soviet troops back in the 1980s. The stunning scenery was crystal clear, and for the most part so was the radio reception. You couldn't find a better spot in all of Afghanistan to rest, take in the spectacular view, and make a quick radio call.

After summoning Shams, I handed my walkie-talkie to him and asked our platoon's RTO (radio man), Jernigan, to tune to the Taliban frequency with the heaviest traffic. Next, I asked Shams to start calling out some of the Taliban names we constantly intercepted. I received a skeptical look from my translator, as we both knew what I was doing was unsavory. That should have prompted me to rethink my idea.

"Shams, I got this," I said, stupidly. "Please do what I say."

Within a few seconds, we heard a voice. I recognized the voice as a Taliban member who frequented what we jokingly called the Taliban Radio Network.

"Muhammad," I said through my very wide-eyed translator. "Muhammad, are you there?" (Names of some Taliban fighters and US troops have been changed.)

While there was silence on the other end of the radio for at least thirty seconds, Jernigan started laughing while Shams looked completely shocked by what I was doing.

"Who is this?" Muhammad said in Pashto, "Why are you calling me?"

"This is Lieutenant Groberg with the United States Army," I said while trying not to laugh. "I have an important message for you.

"The war is over," I continued. "You can now turn in all your weapons at Combat Outpost Honaker-Miracle, and we promise not to shoot at you. Once all the weapons are collected, we will leave your country."

By this point, Shams had joined Jernigan in laughing, which Muhammad could certainly hear in the background.

More silence, until . . .

"You son of shit," Muhammad yelled. "I will crush you and your pig American soldiers."

"Well, thanks for that, Muhammad," I said through Shams. "But that's not very nice."

The laughter blew my cover, and predictably, the enemy fighter was not amused.

"*Inshallah*, we will kill you and then come to America and kill your wives, too," he screamed. "Then we will kill your daughters!"

"Okay, okay, Muhammad, here's Plan B," I said through Shams. "Instead of coming up to Honaker-Miracle, go ahead and give your wives and daughters your weapons, because they are better warriors than you will ever be—"

BOOM.

It was the sound of Taliban RPGs blasting into the side of a snowy mountain that was about two miles to our north in the nearby Watapur Valley, where COP Michigan was located. We could see the smoke and fire from our vantage point, which prompted me to let Muhammad know that his aim was way off.

Suddenly, I got a tap on my shoulder from Martinez.

"Sir, isn't Lieutenant Thompson's platoon on patrol near COP Michigan today?" he said.

Oh shit.

At our nightly post-mission briefing, Saul, who had thankfully made it back to base safely, was drumming through his accounts of the day when he mentioned one in particular.

"One of the Taliban teams—I think it was some idiot low-level fighter—completely exposed his position to us and started shooting RPGs that hit this mountain right above us," he said.

To reiterate, Saul and I were best friends from the University of

Maryland. He was a towering six-foot-five dude with brown hair, a wide smile, and mesmerizing eyes (as women would often say). Ladies flocked to him and he was used to it. In college, we never went to parties at the Greek houses, but instead frequented congested bars so we could catch up and talk about our various fantasy sports leagues while drinking cheap beer. We became brothers long before we were coincidentally deployed together, which only strengthened our bond.

I owed Saul an honest explanation, especially before I got grilled by the boss about what happened outside the wire.

"Um, yeah, about that . . ." I said, my face filling with heat. "So I might have been talking to one of Dairon's guys before that happened, and I might have pissed him off a little bit."

On cue, our CO exploded.

"What did you just say, Groberg?" he yelled. *"What the hell were you thinking?"*

"I'm sorry, sir," I said as my posture straightened.

"I appreciate that, Groberg," he shot back. "But 'sorry' wouldn't really cut it at the funerals of Thompson and his entire God damn platoon," he said, pointing out the obvious.

"No, sir," I said, truly ashamed.

"Thompson, good work out there today," the CO said to Saul before dismissing us with an annoyed look on his face. "Glad your buddy didn't get you shot up."

As I walked out of the TOC behind Saul, I let him know how genuinely sorry I was. Even though I knew him well, Saul's response was nevertheless surprising.

"I thought what you did was awesome," he said with a grin. "Screw these Talis [slang for Taliban] . . . they can kiss my ass."

Through trial and error (after error), I somehow managed to develop a decent daily routine. After waking up at around 0600, I would visit the TOC to get an updated enemy situation and weather report, adjust the day's patrol, and alert platoons stationed on other FOBs and COPs if we planned to cross into any of the zones they were responsible for. Then I would lead a five-minute operations order and mission brief for my platoon before everyone checked their weapons and ultimately loaded up the trucks to go outside the wire. Six days a week, we would leave the COP to confront the enemy and hold meetings with those village elders.

The soldiers under my command had it a lot tougher than I did. While I could retreat to my room at any time to fill out after-action reports or watch movies, those guys were bunking together and, for the most part, were always on duty. Due to the constant threat of enemy attacks, each of the COP's guard towers had to be manned at all times. My men and Thompson's soldiers would rotate in four-hour increments—day or night and whether the temperature was 19 degrees (as it was at this point in the deployment) or 91 degrees. As their leader, I had enormous respect for the sacrifices these young soldiers were making on a daily basis.

While Shams and I were busy negotiating village construction project costs with usually corrupt Afghan contractors, my guys were repairing or cleaning the trucks. While I was working on the next day's mission plan, my married soldiers were calling their wives and children back home. While I was "sleeping in" until 0600, the cooks were waking up at 0430 to make us breakfast. These dedicated, hard-working soldiers were not only every bit as tough as anyone in the Army; they were the unsung heroes of America's wars. Every time I had an extra moment in Afghanistan, I would always remind myself of how lucky I was.

On one particularly chilly morning approximately three weeks into my stint at COP Honaker-Miracle, gunfire erupted from a guard tower. One of the soldiers had allegedly spotted a Chechnyan sniper aiming his Soviet-era Dragunov rifle at us from atop a nearby mountain. We were used to gunfire at our COP, but since it was early in the morning and our snow-covered courtyard was mostly empty, the piercing sounds from our guard's machine gun echoed loudly.

The same sniper had been terrorizing Honaker-Miracle for weeks. Intelligence reports led us to believe that his cave was on the side of a mountain where we were continually dropping bombs, but our actions were ineffective. To my chagrin, these massive explosions—the biggest and loudest I had ever heard—seemed only to be flattening trees and pounding sand and snow in the cliffs. Even though I grudgingly acknowledged that this particular sniper was pretty good at his "job," if you could call it that, I was tired of having to say a Hail Mary every time I walked on open ground around my base.

The sniper's rounds, which were probably provided by al Qaeda, hadn't hit anything on our COP during this particular firefight. After a few minutes of return fire from the guard towers, his rifle went silent.

It was time to act. After I spoke with Saul, we had our best guys jump into our Oshkosh MRAP (Mine Resistant Ambush Protected) M-ATVs (all terrain vehicles), which were still being prepped for the day's mission. These large vehicles are more effective at protecting soldiers from IED blasts than Humvees. Using the same heat signature equipment we relied on during nighttime patrols, our platoon's experts were able to find the sniper cowering in the hills. Within moments, our gunners were raining 120mm mortars down on that location in a cacophony of an assault. No survivors were possible in an attack of this magnitude.

As one thirty-five-pound mortar after another exploded into the valley, we saw no further movement from the hiding spot pinpointed by our heat signature technology. It remained that way until the next day.

Less than twenty-four hours later, a soldier on guard tower duty spotted a large group of unidentified locals gathering near the same ridgeline. Since Islam requires a proper burial as soon as possible from the time of death, I thought to myself that the soldier had probably witnessed the sniper's funeral.

Four days after that attack, my team and I packed up the M-ATVs and headed out to the village closest to the sniper's suspected lair. As a group of us met with the village elder, one of the soldiers on guard duty radioed the TOC to notify them of a very interesting development. A kid had just told him that he and his group of friends had found a sniper rifle.

"Time out," I told my fellow soldiers. "Did anyone just hear that?"

Sure enough, the rifle was a Dragunov, and after we went outside and gave the boy a few pieces of candy, the child confirmed that the funeral we had seen indeed belonged to the sniper. Although we suspected this was the outcome all along, it was a huge relief to have it confirmed.

Instead of giving the boy more candy, which probably would have upset his stomach from eating so many sweets, I pulled a crank radio out of my bag.

"Shams, go give him this," I told my translator. "Also please tell him thank you and *As Salam alaikum*." Peace be upon you.

Because of the sniper's death and continually plummeting temperatures, things got relatively quiet from late December until the end of February. I use the word "relatively" because we still went outside the wire every day for Shuras (meetings held in accordance with the ancient Pashtunwali code) with village elders. We also continued going on daily combat patrols, which became even more tiresome when the already brutal, shaky terrain was covered with several feet of snow. Shockingly, US Army platoons don't get the luxury of snow days.

Even in the winter months, our COP continued taking mortar and RPG fire from what we called the Taliban's "D team," which generally stepped forward while Dairon and his gang vacationed in Pakistan or hibernated in their caves. Their replacements were usually teenagers sent over the eastern border to learn how to fight the barbaric infidels (us). For the most part, these amateurs could barely aim their weapons, let alone strike significant targets. It was nevertheless my job to keep the entire platoon focused and ready in case the D team got lucky and actually hit something.

That dreaded moment arrived on December 25, 2009, when the Taliban blew up the platoon's mail truck, while I was still at FOB Blessing.

If you haven't served in the military, you may not fully understand how important and sacred a mail truck is to a soldier's morale (and sanity). Those trucks bring letters from our loved ones, photos of our newborns, and poems from our children. In truth, they bring us a light at the end of a very dark tunnel. That's why blowing up a mail truck represented a lot more than losing a vehicle. Most devastatingly, it happened on Christmas Day.

After the vehicle fire was put out, soldiers found the remnants of dozens of Christmas care packages that had been assembled with so much love by family members and military charities. The toughest part of that day for my men was sorting through charred photos of their children at Christmastime. Sure, nobody had been killed in the attack, for which we were grateful, but the Taliban still managed to ruin the holiday.

As a single guy who loved watching football, the D team's next successful attack left me just as disheartened. On the morning of the Super Bowl, a Soviet-era mortar managed to hit the chow hall and damage the satellite dish. That night, the cooks had planned a surprise meal for the big game, but instead of watching the New Orleans Saints battle the Indianapolis Colts on February 7, 2010, the soldiers of COP Honaker-Miracle were relegated to playing videogames.

It was a terrible evening until one of our mechanics realized he could repair and reposition the satellite. The mechanics had already saved the day many times by fixing our trucks or Internet connections, but this particular mechanic scored a touchdown for all of us on that memorable night. It felt so good to watch football, eat wings, and forget that we were in Afghanistan.

For all the bullshit we had to deal with in Afghanistan, some days made everything worth it. After being awoken by the Muslim prayer call that resonated through the gradually warming valley every morning (and five times a day), my platoon journeyed along the Pech River to a place called Andersille. That particular village had a kind, honest elder who I learned had been leading the charge against the Soviet Union in Afghanistan while I was being potty trained by my mother in France.

While corruption and mistrust definitely existed in many Afghan villages, individuals like this gentle old man, Ahmed, reminded me that while there were many bad actors in Kunar Province, the ordinary Afghans were good, caring people. Through no fault of their own, citizens of the historic land where I was deployed lived in a much more primitive culture than the civilized world I was used to.

After exchanging pleasantries about a visit my platoon had made to one of the village's schools the previous week, Ahmed formally began the Shura with the traditional *As Salam alaikum*. We called these visits key leader engagements (KLEs). They were among our platoon's most important duties in Afghanistan.

As usual, Ahmed began by pouring me a cup of chai or tea. The cup was dirty and the tea tasted like a mixture of Pepto-Bismol and soil, but not to drink the entire cup would have been viewed as extremely disrespectful under the Pashtunwali code. Therefore, I sipped the chai while displaying my best poker face.

I had a hard and fast rule about KLEs being no longer than thirty minutes. Not only did that prevent the villagers from asking me for everything under the sun, but it also protected my soldiers, who were pulling security outside the village gates—a position in which they were often shot at.

Ahmed genuinely appreciated all that the Americans had done and were doing for his village, and seemed to sincerely care about me and my soldiers. He even asked whether any of us had children, which I appreciated. Three-plus months after arriving in eastern Afghanistan, Ahmed was the only elder who seemed to fully understand what my men were sacrificing each day to help the men, women, and children of his village and others.

"Thank you for visiting the All-Boys School last week, Lieutenant," Ahmed said through Shams. "If you don't mind, I have one more request."

Oh, here it comes. Just as I was starting to like Ahmed, he was probably about to ask the Army for a month's worth of fuel and/or a new retaining wall.

"This is a historic invitation, Lieutenant," he continued to my surprise. "I would like you to visit our village's All-Girls School."

Wow. Not only had I completely misjudged Ahmed's motives, for which I felt deeply embarrassed, but he didn't need to explain the significance of this forthcoming event for me to understand its symbolism. Other than an elder or teacher, it was strictly forbidden for any male—let alone an armed US Army soldier—to enter an All-Girls School.

"I am deeply honored by your request," I had Shams tell Ahmed. "It is with great humility and appreciation that I accept."

The next day, I was greeted by the smiling faces of little girls ranging in age from six to twelve years old. Their prominent, mostly hazel eyes seemed wider than American children's eyes, perhaps because they had witnessed so much war and suffering at such a young age.

"My name is Flo Groberg," I told about forty young students after Ahmed gave me permission to speak to them. "I used to live in France, but now I am a soldier from the United States of America."

Before Shams could finish translating, one little girl—probably about eight years old—stood up. To my complete shock, she spoke to me in English.

"Are you here to hurt us?" she inquired pointedly.

"No," I whispered while kneeling down to speak with her. "My soldiers and I are here to protect you and to help your moms and dads."

It was hard not to dwell on that question, or feel heartbroken while looking at the faces of these innocent children. They had grown up in the most dangerous valley of a country that had already been at war for a decade when they were born. While I didn't have kids of my own, the concept of a little girl growing up in a rugged, primordial place like Afghanistan—where women were sometimes murdered, raped, and oppressed—bordered on the unimaginable.

At the same time, the fact that these girls were being taught English was *deeply* inspiring. To me, nothing underscored the importance of what the men in my platoon were risking on a daily basis more than that school visit.

Speaking to those little girls was the single best moment of my first deployment to Afghanistan. I will never forget the mixture of curiosity and fear in their eyes, or what the same English-speaking girl asked me after I was given permission to hug her.

"Please keep us safe from the bad men," she said while tugging on my green and brown combat fatigues.

"I promise that I will," I said while looking squarely into her eyes.

A few days after the school visit, I took my platoon out to visit a different school in Shege, where I had fallen into the river of shit earlier in the deployment. We went back because I was determined to visit the village elder—the one I had previously berated—to make amends.

For three hours, we handed out candy and school supplies to the same kids we would often see collecting brass from spent ammunition during our many violent firefights. We also decided to play soccer with a bunch of young boys, who were silly with excitement. It was a great way to start the day.

We returned at about 1400, and by 1500 I was working out in our base's small gym when I heard a jarring series of explosions. It only took me a second or two to realize that I was hearing the loud echoes of exploding enemy RPGs and mortars.

About a minute or so later, Martinez hurried into the gym.

"Lieutenant . . . Thompson and the CO are waiting for you in the TOC," he said.

Saul and our commanding officer told me that a patrol that included our battalion commander, Lieutenant Colonel Pearl, was on its way to the city of Asadabad—the capital of Kunar Province—when it was attacked. The explosions that rang through the gym were echoing from an area close to COP Able Main, along the Pech River, but about a mile to our west.

"Get out there and help," my CO said. "Make sure the BC is good to go."

My platoon's role as Quick Reaction Force was to handle the rapid response of the developing situation.

We were on high alert as our trucks carefully plodded along the river toward the village of Mulkhana, near COP Able Main. Though we had passed by this village many times before, we had never taken enemy fire. We assumed that was because the village was right next to a relatively large Afghan police station. A few guys inside our two platoons actually referred to Mulkhana as Shangri-La since it was one of the few relatively safe places in the valley.

We were driving on an unsteady road about five minutes from the village when I noticed something in the distance.

"Stop here," I told my driver, Sergeant Mauldin. "Look up toward that ridgeline. What do you see?"

The sky was blue that day and the glistening sun was reflecting off the Pech River and straight into my eyes. Fortunately, my sunglasses and a lot of squinting helped me identify what I thought was a bunch of Taliban fighters with their weapons pointed downward.

"Ten-Four, L-T," Mauldin said after a few seconds. "I see them."

As I decided what to do next, we heard sounds of return fire, presumably from the BC's boxed-in platoon.

"Go," I told Mauldin while pointing in the other platoon's direction.

About a minute later, we heard a series of booms that sounded as if they were coming from Able Main.

By the time we reached the ambushed patrol, the exchange of fire had stopped. We made a beeline toward the battalion commander, who was sitting inside a military vehicle riddled with bullet holes.

"Sir, Dagger Four-Six is here to support you," I said to LTC Pearl.

"Ten-Four, Lieutenant . . . thanks for getting out here so fast," he said. "We got into a good firefight with those dudes on the ridgeline before we called for a fire artillery mission."

He then pointed toward Mulkhana's All-Girls School, which was similar to the one I previously visited in Andersille.

"Mortars were fired at the enemy from your COP, " the battalion commander continued. "Unfortunately, one of them came up short."

I didn't even need to ask my boss what he meant before my heart sank. If school had just let out and the mortar came up short, then it almost certainly landed among the young girls departing to their homes.

"I know this is going to be tough, Lieutenant, but I need you to take your men into the village and take pictures of any civilian casualties, and then bring back the elder," he said with his head down. "We'll need all of this for the investigation."

Was he serious? While I understood why the Army needed to document such a tragic event, I was nevertheless shocked that I'd just been ordered to take my men into a hostile village, take photographs of dead children, and bring the village elder back to where we were.

Approaching the school, I felt worse than I had ever felt. To my horror, I found two dead bodies upon my arrival. They were covered with dirt and blood-soaked shrouds.

I felt convulsions in my neck and chest as I saw the bodies and heard the sounds of devastated villagers. Dozens of people were crying, but many more were pointing and yelling in my platoon's direction. That's when Sergeant Dement, a young NCO in my platoon who had served in Iraq and always managed to stay composed during the worst possible situations, went to work on easing the tensions between the locals and my soldiers.

"Please step back so my leader can talk to yours," he said while gently waving his arms. "We are here to help and to find out what happened."

As the elder approached a minute later, I told my soldiers—who were also deeply affected by what they had seen but also on guard for possible reprisal attacks—to temporarily lower their weapons.

"I am terribly sorry for your loss," I told this quiet village elder—whom I had never met—through Shams. "My men and I just got here, but we want to give you our deepest condolences after this tragic accident."

He didn't say anything in response. Recognizing the delicacy of a sad but also potentially dangerous situation for my men, I carefully explained that I needed to take photographs of both bodies in order to ensure that my government could properly investigate the matter and compensate the families of both little girls.

The elder, who seemed strangely unmoved by the dreadful scene, obliged.

As the bodies were uncovered, blood rushed from my face and left me pale. One girl had a perfect face, untouched by the carnage, but her body no longer resembled that of a human being. The second child's body was intact and looked unharmed, but her face had been scarred by war.

In a sickening, surreal moment that blurred the lines between humanity and civil duty, I began to snap pictures. As I documented the horrendous images that the Army ordered me to capture, I felt like I had failed every innocent child living in this vicious hellhole.

"Hey American," the elder said in Pashto while interrupting my mind-numbing task. "You also killed one of my cows."

After my eyes met with my translator's, I couldn't really figure out what to say in response. Instead, I shrugged my shoulders as if to say "so what?"

"You need to pay me for the cow," the elder said.

I tightened my lips and shook my head. *Did he just say what I thought he said?*

"Who cares about the cow?" I said to Shams, not understanding the animal's significance. "What about the two girls?"

"One of them is my granddaughter," the elder said, to my complete astonishment. "You need to give me one thousand dollars for my girl and ten thousand dollars for my cow."

In that moment, all the goodwill from the recent Shuras and school visits evaporated into thin air. The elder was asking for ten times more in compensation for the cow's death than his granddaughter's.

I wanted to punch him in the face, but instead I just walked away. I told Shams to have the elder follow us back to the vehicle so he could negotiate with my battalion commander instead of me. There was no way I was going to put the lives of my men in further peril in order to debate how much a farm animal was worth versus the life of a child.

As we drove back to Honaker-Miracle, I removed my helmet and bowed my head into my sweaty hands. When I slumped down in my truck's passenger seat, I saw the dead child's mutilated face. Her face would return to haunt me many times.

5   HONAKER-MIRACLE

I should have died several times in Afghanistan, but one day in 2010 in particular stands out.

It was springtime and the Taliban "A team," led by Dairon, was back. Instead of enjoying the gradually warming temperatures, the soldiers at COP Honaker-Miracle were rewarded by daily increases in rocket-propelled grenade attacks, which were getting more and more accurate as the enemy regained its rhythm. As sure as the sun rose over the lofty mountains, whatever semblance of peace our small base enjoyed in the winter was now officially over.

My platoon was on its way back from Shege village on an otherwise pleasant afternoon when my CO contacted our M-ATV over the radio.

"Dagger-Four-Six, I need you to escort a clip to COP Michigan and then FOB Blessing," he said while adding that Afghan soldiers were on their way to "help" us.

Receiving this order sucked on multiple levels. "Clip" was the nickname for a convoy of fuel trucks, which would make us sitting ducks for the Taliban and their RPGs. Going to Blessing also meant that our large vehicles would have to lumber almost six miles along the river and through the lethal valley just to deliver some fuel.

To make things even more complicated, we would have to escort a convoy of Afghan National Army vehicles along with us.

When the ANA convoy arrived, I stopped them and began embedding each vehicle into our patrol: first, an American truck, then two Afghan vehicles, a fuel truck, and two more Afghan vehicles, then my truck, then the second fuel truck, and so on. In total, there were three fuel trucks, four American vehicles, and six Afghan trucks.

Before we set out on a perilous journey, I confronted the ANA commander.

"Look, we have three fuel trucks in this patrol that are essentially powder kegs waiting to blow us all up," I said to him through Shams. "That means we have to push through no matter what happens.

"My soldiers and I will come back to fight these guys later," I continued. "But whatever happens out there: *do not stop.*"

As my translator relayed the message, the Afghan commander nodded his head and insisted that he understood.

"Okay, no problem, very good, very good," he continually repeated.

We were slowly passing a dangerous area along the Pech river we called Turali when three consecutive RPGs—aimed straight at the fuel trucks—roared down from the mountains. All we could do for the next few seconds was hold our breath.

"They missed!" yelled one of my gunners, Richardson.

"Speed up and let's get out of here," I said while breathing a quick sigh of relief.

As soon as Mauldin's foot hit the gas pedal, the two Afghan vehicles in front of ours stopped dead.

It took only a split second—which is all the time you have in a firefight—for my confusion to morph into unbridled rage. Adrenaline helped me push open my M-ATV's heavy door as the Afghan commander ran up alongside our vehicle and started banging on it.

"WHAT ARE YOU DOING, DUDE?" I yelled as he stared at me in shock. "I TOLD YOU NOT TO STOP!"

I then yelled toward Shams.

"Tell him to get back in his damn truck and to stop being scared," I screamed loud enough to ensure that Shams would hear me amid the chaos. "GO!"

Shams translated, but the Afghan commander kept standing still, paralyzed by fear.

With the likelihood of a follow-up RPG attack increasing by the second, I had no choice but to act. As all four American vehicles blasted the mountain with a massive amount of return fire, I dismounted from my truck and grabbed the ANA commander's left arm. I tried to stay calm as I looked him in the eyes.

"You have to trust me," I said. "If we stay here, we are going to lose people."

I then pointed toward his truck.

"Go back!" I said while raising my voice.

There was *still* no response. With a duty to protect my men, I dragged the commander through the crossfire and threw him back into his truck. My actions surprised his fellow Afghan soldiers, who were sitting there doing nothing.

"We've got to go!" I said to the ANA commander before ducking behind his truck to avoid getting shot.

Following a sprint back to my M-ATV, I ordered my men to quickly light up the mountain with missiles and MK 19 grenades, which would complement their already furious .50 caliber machine gun fire. Suddenly, the ridgeline submerged in gigantic mushroom clouds of smoke.

Moments later, the enemy stopped returning fire. We weren't sure if our foes were alive or dead, but either way we had to get the heck out of there before they hit one of those fuel trucks and turned all of us into a Fourth of July barbecue. About a minute later, the Afghan trucks ahead of us finally started to move.

When we arrived to drop off fuel at our first stop, COP Michigan,

I got out of the truck. I was still very angry with the Afghan soldier, who was probably given his command because of his stature in a local clan, which was often the case in the Afghan National Army. Unlike Americans, ANA soldiers almost never receive proper training unless we give it to them.

"Commander, I need you to understand that you simply *cannot stop* when you get scared," I said as SFC Staley lurked nearby to make sure I didn't lose my temper. "That's how people die. Let's not do that on the way to Blessing, okay?"

A few minutes later, we proceeded with our patrol and dropped off the ANA convoy safely at FOB Blessing. Then we had to turn right back around and—once again—push through Turali.

As we approached this dangerous area for a second time, the warm afternoon sun was glistening off the Pech River.

"Coming up on Turali," I said over the radio. "We don't know how many of these guys we got last time, so be ready for anything."

That was one of the biggest challenges about serving in this part of Afghanistan. Even after unloading hundreds upon hundreds of missiles, bombs, and bullets in a given hotspot, you usually wouldn't know whether you actually took out the enemy.

Things were unusually quiet as Richardson scanned Turali using his joystick-controlled viewer, which I could also see on my separate command screen. After finding nothing, my eyes wandered toward the passenger's window and beyond a nearby police station to the seemingly endless mountain scenery. In an attempt to calm my racing heartbeat, I took a deep breath while adjusting my perpetually uncomfortable heavy body armor.

Another soldier named Moffett, who was also scanning Turali, then broke my stare with six emphatic words.

"We are about to get hit," he yelled.

While zooming in on the police station, Moffett had seen an Afghan policeman looking at the ridgeline to our north with binoculars while talking on his phone. As was all too common with the Afghan police force, he was probably working (or being forced to work) with the Taliban, and was therefore relaying our precise position to the enemy.

I was frantically scanning the riverbank for threats when a terrifying shadow appeared less than fifty feet from my window. I will never forget the sight of the rugged, bearded Taliban fighter popping up from behind a rock while holding a rocket launcher on his shoulder. It was aimed squarely at my face.

This was the moment of my death. I was sure of it.

I was just starting to warn my men of the looming rocket when I heard the unmistakable scream of an RPG being fired. As the terrible sound echoed through my ears, there was nothing left to do except shut my eyes.

My limbs tensed and my mind went blank. My heart rate slowed as I recognized that it was neither fight nor flight. All that was left for my men and me was to be at peace with our demise.

I thought of my Uncle Abdou. Even though I was about to be killed in Afghanistan at a young age, I thought, at least I had done everything in my power to avenge his death, as well as the deaths of many innocent Americans who lost their lives on 9/11. I saw the RPG coming directly at me.

Just as it was about to make contact, I blacked out.

A miracle occurred that day on the banks of the Pech River when the Taliban fighter's RPG faltered.

Instead of crashing through our vehicle and blowing up four American soldiers, the RPG instead hit the top of the frame of the very window I was looking out of. It then bounced straight up in the air, detonating above us.

I was jolted back to consciousness when our vehicle shook from the explosion.

"Holy shit!" my driver yelled as the detonation rattled the M-ATV's windows and the pits of our stomachs. "Smoke that guy, Richardson!"

Staying as calm as he could in a life-or-death moment, Richardson quickly found the enemy fighter, who was running away, on his screen. After adjusting his joystick, he pressed the red button and fired.

Just as the lethal .50 cal rounds were about to hit him in the back, the Taliban fighter turned around—seemingly on cue—and looked at us. The rounds struck him in the chest and blew his body apart.

As pieces of this man's body flew in the air, I heard cheering. I recognize that it must be strange and rather sickening to read about a bunch of guys celebrating a man's gruesome death, but having just survived a terrifying attack, we cheered.

The near-death experience shook me up, and both Moffett and Richardson knew it. After we were in the clear, they started reminding me over the radio that the threat had been eliminated.

"We got him, sir," Richardson said.

"Thanks for saving our asses," I said. Those were the only words I could muster while my mind came to grips with the fact that I wasn't dreaming. Somehow, we had all made it out of Turali without suffering a single scratch.

By the grace of the same God who spared our lives, the rest of the drive back to Honaker-Miracle was uneventful. As we ate dinner together on the base, I realized that all of my men—not just me— were at a loss for words.

"Close call out there today," Staley said in a monotone voice accompanied by a wry smirk.

Honestly, what else was there to say? For some reason, we had escaped an insane situation that should have put us all inside flag-draped caskets on a C-130 bound for Dover Air Force Base in Delaware.

For the next five minutes, I enjoyed the hot dog I was eating in our tiny chow hall. The cliché of feeling "lucky to be alive" was more real than ever as my soldiers and I shared that moment as friends and brothers. We had all been given a second chance.

By the first night of April, my vivid nightmares about the dead Afghan girls were getting worse. In one particular dream, I was kneeling over one of the girls' bodies when she woke up, grabbed my body armor, and asked why I didn't keep my promise to help the innocent children of Afghanistan.

Just as I was about to tell the little girl that I was sorry, a jarring knock on the door jolted me out of my sleep.

"Sir, permission to enter?" the voice on the other side of the door requested.

I was upset, confused, and half asleep when I trudged through the dust, answered the door, and saw the face of one of my platoon's youngest soldiers.

"What do you want, man?" I said. "It's 0530."

"Sir, Lieutenant Thompson has been hit," he said.

What?

I'm not sure if this soldier realized that I had known Saul since our University of Maryland days and that he was one of my best friends. Hazily, I ordered the young man to go back outside my door, count to five, knock again, and repeat the news.

"If you are playing an April Fool's joke on me, I swear I'm gonna kick your ass," I said.

Sure enough, five seconds later, the rookie soldier knocked a second time.

"Sir . . . Lieutenant Thompson has been hit," he slowly repeated.

For the first time in Afghanistan, I panicked.

"What's his status?" I yelled.

"I don't know, sir," he said. "I'm sorry, sir."

Seeing the fear in my fellow soldier's face made me realize how serious the situation was.

"Shit," I said while scrambling to put on my uniform. Less than two minutes later, I ran out the door toward the TOC.

Saul was the Taliban's most wanted American in the Pech River Valley. That's because Dairon and his gang had seen him in action and surmised that Saul was the most skilled, most talented infantry officer in the region. Knowing how big a target was already on Saul's back made the news I had just received all the more terrifying.

As I stepped into the TOC, everyone was standing around the radio listening to what was happening on top of the mountain where Saul had been hit. It still wasn't clear if he was all right.

All I wanted to hear was Saul's voice. After what felt like an eternity, the radio crackled.

"Hey, Phil, hit that OP right now!" Saul screamed on the radio.

Saul was alive! Incredibly, as I would learn, he had survived an RPG landing *between his legs.* It was just one of those crazy things that happened in combat. I knew that my friend was tough, but this was pure luck.

Saul however, was seriously wounded in the attack. His arms and legs were soaked in blood from shrapnel that had pierced sections of his body armor. Fortunately, the explosion's deadly upward pattern had stopped just before reaching his heart and neck. Amazingly, especially considering where the RPG landed, Saul's manhood was also intact.

Knowing Saul, a six-foot-five American warrior whose platoon probably killed more Taliban than any other soldiers in the valley that year, I was sure he would be back on the battlefield in a few days.

As radio traffic confirmed that a helicopter was carrying my injured friend to safety, any remaining feelings of invincibility that I had were gone. Even though nobody in my platoon or Saul's had been killed since my arrival in Afghanistan, there had now been many—too many—close calls for comfort. In that moment, I realized that surviving combat is probably more about luck than anything else.

Six days later, as Afghanistan's notorious summer fighting season approached, Saul was back on top of the very mountain where he had nearly been killed. This time, the enemy was determined to finish the job.

The Taliban had surrounded his platoon with multiple fighters and was raining hell down on Saul and his soldiers. Cool, calm, and collected, Saul ordered his men to take a defensive posture. Still, with continuous AK-47 rounds hitting the trees and rocks all around them, Saul knew that he needed support.

As soon as word reached COP Honaker-Miracle that Saul was pinned down, we sprang to action.

"Groberg, get your ass in the TOC," screamed our executive officer, First Lieutenant Fio Rito, who was second in command to the CO. He then told me that we were going to be Saul's Quick Reaction Force and that we had to be out the door as soon as possible.

"What the hell is going on, sir?" I asked. "Where's Saul at?"

"Same spot as last time," Rito said. "Except today, the enemy came ready to fight."

After the jarring news, I ran as fast as I could to inform Staley of the situation.

"Saul is in it again . . . we need to be out the gate in twenty minutes as QRF," I told Staley. "Get the boys ready."

"Roger," Staley answered in his typically stoic manner.

In twenty minutes, we had four trucks out the gate to set out on one of our riskiest journeys of the deployment. To get to Saul, we would have to travel through unstable terrain that included a creek and a dirt road that was never meant to support the weight of our trucks. This was our only route into this section of the valley, so we had no choice but to proceed toward the danger.

Because of the vicious terrain, it took us over forty minutes just to enter the valley where Saul had started his ascent up the mountain.

As we entered the valley, I noticed our TOW (tube-launched, optically tracked, wire-guided) missile truck shaking more than ever before.

"I think the ground is going to give out," I screamed at my driver. *"Go left!"*

Just as I started yelling, everything below us seemed to evaporate. Before I could blink, my men and I were cursing in fear as our truck rolled into the river.

There was silence for a split second as we waited for the sounds of water rushing into our vehicle.

"Sir, we need to get out of this truck through the gunner's hatch . . . right now," my driver screamed.

"Roger that. Cortez, you go first," I said. "Shams, you are next, then you (the driver). I'll go last."

I don't think I ever saw four men move that quickly as the nightmarish scenario began to unfold. Like many other soldiers, drowning was one of my worst fears. That is *not* the way I wanted to go out, and I'm sure my soldiers felt the same way.

Despite panic, all those years of Army training quickly set in. After my three fellow passengers exited safely, I dismounted our multimillion-dollar TOW missile vehicle stuck in the chilly creek.

Just when I thought the situation couldn't get any worse, I began hearing radio chatter about the Taliban redirecting their positions. Instead of continuing to fight Saul's platoon, they were headed straight toward us after hearing that an American vehicle was stuck. We were all alone and an easy target, they must have thought.

By the time the bad guys arrived, I had already managed to call Honaker-Miracle to ask for a "wrecker"—a massive tow truck—and a team of expert soldiers that could get us out of this mess.

As they had done several times before, these brilliant Army mechanics saved my ass and somehow pulled our vehicle out of the creek just before the Taliban arrived. This turn of events made the Taliban so angry that they decided to attack Honaker-Miracle instead.

To that attack, we responded by firing five TOW missiles, which cost $250,000 *each*. Add in fifty mortars, and the Taliban beat a rapid (and humiliating) retreat. Instead of killing a bunch of Americans, they accomplished nothing.

After we returned to Honaker-Miracle I played cards with Saul and some of his men later that night. Then I stopped by the TOC to see if there was any intercepted radio traffic from the immediate aftermath of the day's harrowing events. Sure enough, there was.

"*Allahu Akbar*, the American devils are dead," a Taliban fighter chanted while clearly referencing the day's fight. "*Inshallah*, we will kill twenty more like them tomorrow."

I couldn't help but smirk as I read the transcripts. At the same time, it was clear that without the heroism of my fellow soldiers, the enemy fighter's lies could have just as easily come true. As was often the case, things could have turned out much differently if the mechanics hadn't responded so quickly.

By May, I think that most of the village elders began to genuinely respect my platoon, even when we refused to hire more contractors for construction projects or to risk our lives to protect a clip of fuel funded by American taxpayers. If there was one takeaway for the local leaders during my deployment, it was that Afghans need to ask the *Afghan* government for help, not Uncle Sam.

Even as the number of firefights increased as the summer season approached, I still felt like we were winning our protracted battle with Dairon and the Taliban. In addition to killing one hundred (or more) Taliban fighters, we successfully closed COP Michigan and completed the Pentagon-ordered withdrawal from the violent Korengal Valley, which had become familiar to some Americans because of Sebastian Junger and Tim Hetherington's visceral 2010 documentary *Restrepo*.

For the last few weeks, our most frequent assignment had been to protect the clips carrying fuel, munitions, and other equipment from those shuttered American bases. Once the millions of dollars' worth of items arrived in Jalalabad, the materials would usually be shipped back to military bases in Europe or the United States.

While escorting one such clip along the riverbank between COPs Honaker-Miracle and Able Main, I noticed a tough-looking Afghan staring down at us from the ridgeline near the village of Shamir Kowtz. I squinted, trying to determine whether he was carrying a weapon.

"Yo, Cortez, look at this dude," I said. "I can't see much, but he looks bad."

Cortez, who was manning the TOW missile system, agreed. Still, there was nothing we could do due to our rules of engagement. Even though we operated under a steady threat of enemy ambushes, I couldn't order an Afghan to his death simply because he looked suspicious, even if we were patrolling an active combat zone.

All of us were zeroed in on the possible bad guy when suddenly we heard the rear hatch of our M-ATV swing open. Simultaneously, the heads of every American soldier in the stopped vehicle whipped around as all four of us tried to figure out what the hell was going on.

It wasn't the Taliban trying to breach our truck, but a bunch of

Afghan boys stealing everything they could get their hands on, from ammunition to medical equipment.

"What the hell, Cortez?" I screamed. "You didn't see a group of kids running toward our vehicle?"

"You told me to check out the guy on the ridgeline, L-T!" said Cortez, who was absolutely right. We were focused on the threat, not the back of our mammoth military truck.

By this time in my deployment, I should have known that this sequence of events was probably happening by design. The Taliban had most likely paid those kids to distract us just long enough to move their men into position for an assault.

Without fully pondering the possibility of an ambush, I ordered my men to dismount and enter Shamir Kowtz, where we found the village elder sitting in a rocking chair.

"We're going to a play a game," I said to the elder. "It's called 'you tell those kids to give us our stuff back—'"

Before I could finish, the thundering sounds of machine gun fire erupted.

"Shit!" Martinez yelled as our four-man team quickly spread out, as we had been trained to do.

Seconds later, a dozen or so machine gun rounds pounded the dirt directly in front of me, getting closer and closer to my legs as the gunfire continued to roar. Without thinking, I sprinted toward the first structure to my right as the rounds kept getting closer to our feet.

Fortunately, none of us were hit, but by this point our nine lives were disappearing at a drastic rate.

"Dement, you good?" I asked

"Good to go, sir!" he responded.

"Richardson and Moffett . . . y'all good?" I asked next.

"Yup! We are fine," Richardson said back. "Anyone see where it's coming from?"

Of course not, I thought. These Taliban guys were like ghosts; they blended in with the terrain, and today they had a plan.

Once the enemy fire died down, I moved behind a big rock to get a better vantage point. Using the rock as cover, I shot more rounds out of my rifle that day than all previous firefights in Afghanistan combined.

Upon realizing that where I had been shooting probably wasn't the location of the enemy, I repositioned our trucks to better identify their location. As Staley led the show from our vehicles, he finally pinpointed a possible position and called in a fire mission. Ten minutes and twelve mortar rounds later, the enemy resumed their attack; this time with a bit more anger behind it.

My platoon exchanged fire with the enemy for the next four hours until the Taliban eventually stopped returning fire. Unlike a movie, there was no dramatic climax to the battle—just silence, which usually meant that we had won.

When we caught our breath and returned to our still open M-ATV, the crystal clear weather of that particular day enabled us to see the bodies of three Taliban fighters on the cliff. We were probably fighting five guys in total judging by the gunfire I heard, which meant that we killed most of their team before the others ran away. Due to the firefight's chaos, my platoon didn't know exactly who had killed the bad guys, but considering that we had been caught off guard by the enemy attack, I would say things turned out pretty damn well.

"Now that was fun, L-T," said Sergeant Dement.

He was right, even though that line of machine gun fire had come far too close to hitting me. Escaping that huge firefight unscathed reinforced how fortunate each of us felt by that point in our combat tour.

Even the Taliban fighter who falsely claimed to have killed "American devils" in the past couldn't spin this one. I read about him lamenting our latest Houdini act in a subsequent radio transcript.

"These American shits have an invisible shield," he said.

If you looked down on the Pech River Valley during almost any day of that deployment, you would have seen a crescendo of explosions resembling the opening sequence of *Apocalypse Now*. Indeed, the US Army expended more ordnance in our area of operations in 2009 and 2010 than all other bases in Afghanistan *combined*.

From the dead of winter to the dawn of summer fighting season, we had spent the last seven months—and more than a year in the case of the soldiers serving under me—in what was truly the most dangerous place on earth. My tour was 217 days long, and in that time frame, we engaged with the enemy more than two hundred times.

Just before Memorial Day, we made one of our last fuel clip escorts to FOB Blessing. That's when I got a radio call from a female Kiowa helicopter pilot who was watching our patrol from the skies above the dreaded valley.

"Dagger-Four-Six this is Unfair-Three-Six, I see two enemy fighters approaching your clip holding what appear to be AK-47s, over," she said. "Request permission to engage, over."

"Unfair-Three-Six this is Dagger-Four-Six . . . permission granted," I radioed back.

BOOM. BOOM. The pilot fired two rockets that sent plumes of fire and smoke shooting into the bright blue sky from a nearby cornfield.

"This is Unfair-Three-Six . . . target expired," she calmly reported over the radio. "Over and out."

The soldier who had saved us from yet another Taliban ambush was landing her Kiowa helicopter to refuel just as our clip arrived to FOB Blessing. As she disembarked and removed her helmet, her long blond hair was blowing in the wind.

"Wow!" the entire platoon—no exaggeration—collectively gasped.

Even though we had been betting each other on what she looked like for the entire ride to Blessing, none of us were bold enough to ask the pilot for her name. Still, as 4th Platoon, Dagger Company's violent chapter in Afghanistan's Pech River Valley finally came to a close, I was convinced that she was an angel. As I would later tell Saul over margaritas on a wild post-deployment vacation to Mexico, divine intervention is the only explanation for how the boys of Combat Outpost Honaker-Miracle were able to survive those seven months of hell.

Shortly after my platoon left Afghanistan, the Pentagon decided to pull all US military forces out of the Pech River Valley. That might lead some to say that my men and I fought for nothing, which would prompt me to argue that they are wrong. My soldiers and I spent every single day serving and sacrificing in the hopes of making life better for ordinary Afghans like the children I met at the Andersille All-Girls School.

This tour, I learned a lot about the fragility of human life. For the first time, I also witnessed the atrocities of war and how they can impact the local populace, and most important, our soldiers. I also learned how to save lives by hunting down the enemy and providing the locals with humanitarian aid. My only regret was not being able to take out Dairon, who was still roaming those deadly hills when I left despite our best efforts to kill him.

My most important mission in Afghanistan was accomplished, which left me feeling elated. After years of training and a lifetime's worth of good luck, I had successfully led a combat platoon through one of the most kinetic environments in the world. Even if I died the next day, I would do so knowing that I helped twenty-four American soldiers come home safely to their families. My men had done the same for me, and for the rest of our lives we would all be brothers-in-arms.

A few months after returning from that raucous south-of-the-border vacation, I got the surprise of a lifetime. Less than two years after leaving the most dangerous place on earth, Uncle Sam would be sending me back.

6 FINISH STRONG

When I landed at Bagram Airfield in February 2012, the US military's image had reached a low point in Afghanistan. That month, NATO International Security Assistance Force troops stationed at Bagram had inadvertently burned forty-eight copies of the Quran that had been removed from a prisoner holding facility.

"I assure you—I promise you—this was not intentional in any way," our commander in Afghanistan, Marine Corps General John Allen, told the Afghan people in a video statement. "I offer my sincere apologies for any offense this may have caused."

Despite General Allen's heartfelt apology and subsequent written statement, much of Afghanistan went nuts. As a February 21, 2012, *New York Times* story put it, "about two thousand Afghans descended on the largest American air base in their country in the bitter cold to protest what is generally regarded as one of the most offensive acts in the Muslim world."

"Protest" was a mild way to characterize what was happening at Bagram as gasoline bomb explosions and "Death to America" chants rattled through the walls of our base. After more than a week of rioting across Afghanistan, according to Associated Press figures, six US troops and at least thirty Afghans were killed. Hundreds more were injured.

No American soldier I knew would ever intentionally burn a Quran. From the start, I firmly believed that this was an unfortunate accident and took General Allen at his word that a full investigation would take place. That still didn't change the fact that people were dying, or that my second tour in Afghanistan was starting under the same persistent, grave threat of violence that surrounded my first deployment.

"Here we go again," I whispered after being briefed on the riots.

Most of my time between deployments had been spent training at Colorado's Fort Carson. After being promoted from second lieutenant to first lieutenant in 2011, I was assigned to the Army's 4th Infantry Division in Afghanistan as the 4th Infantry Brigade Combat Team's personal security detachment commander.

I was now part of Task Force Mountain Warrior, after deploying as a member of Dagger Company the first time around in Afghanistan. Somehow, I always managed to end up in units with badass-sounding names. That is, opposed to some of the other options, which included "Golden Acorn" and "Broken Television," which the 3rd Infantry Division was infamously nicknamed because of a shoulder patch resembling a television with a static screen.

Despite ongoing tensions over the Quran disaster, I felt much safer during my second deployment. That's because my job—coordinating all air and ground movements for my boss, Colonel James Mingus, was much different than my first tour. Instead of near-constant mountain clashes with the Taliban, I was mostly protecting important US and Afghan officials as they traveled to and from meetings. While there were occasional moments of peril, the mission as a whole was like night and day compared to those crazy seven months at COP Honaker-Miracle.

Interestingly enough, the five provinces where we held high-level key leader engagement meetings—Northern and Southern Kunar, Nangarhar, Paktika, Nuristan, and Laghman—included the

Pech River Valley in Kunar province. I visited there often, in fact, even though I was stationed at FOB Fenty in Jalalabad, a major city in Nangarhar province near the Pakistani border. That's where our headquarters for the eastern region of Afghanistan was located.

Whenever I flew by helicopter to FOB Blessing, it stirred up quite a few emotions in me. It felt different, as if decades had passed instead of eighteen months. The sights, sounds, and smells were familiar, yet at the same time it was abundantly clear that this place wasn't anything like what I remembered. Blessing, which Pentagon officials had decided to abandon shortly after I left Afghanistan in the spring of 2010, had been almost completely destroyed by the same Taliban fighters my previous platoon had been trying to kill.

At the time of my departure, FOB Blessing, which my COP Honaker-Miracle–based platoon had visited most frequently, was a bustling American-led facility with a nice gym, shops, housing posts, and an airfield. Less than two years later, it looked like a bomb had gone off inside, which it probably had. As soon as American forces left, enemy fighters swept in and took everything, including toilets and even tiles from the bathroom floor.

"That didn't take long," I said to a fellow soldier, shaking my head.

Forward Operating Base Blessing's rapid demise underscored how much things had changed in eastern Afghanistan since my last deployment. As mentioned, officials in Washington had also decided to leave the rocky, pine-tree-filled Korengal Valley, where more than fifty brave US troops had been killed between 2004 and 2010. That decision led to the Taliban seizing firm control of the mountainous area.

North of Korengal had been COP Michigan, which my company helped to close before leaving the first time. That abandoned COP, which was smack in between Blessing and Honaker-Miracle, was now also under Taliban control after all the sacrifices platoons like mine and Saul's had made in the area.

There were no plans to reopen COP Michigan, but a decision had been made to clean up and refurnish FOB Blessing, where a new group of US soldiers would soon be stationed. In a few short months, American troops serving in eastern Afghanistan would be tasked with winning back the same treacherous territory that so many courageous Americans had fought and bled to secure.

These orders originated from well above my rank and pay grade, so I tried not to waste any time being pissed off about them. I definitely cared, but this action wasn't my primary mission on this deployment. I had no doubt that a good friend of mine, Captain Miller, would succeed while working under the direction of another US Army officer, Captain Ryan, to rebuild FOB Blessing so that US and Afghan soldiers wouldn't be living in miserable conditions.

Another major event had occurred while I was back at Fort Carson: the US military had conducted a major bombing raid to kill Dairon. But instead of eliminating this constant nuisance once and for all, we managed to enrage him further when the blasts killed several members of his family, but not him. Intelligence reports indicated that while Dairon was indeed back in the Pech River Valley, his stature within Taliban ranks had diminished after my platoon's and Saul's hard-fought efforts in 2009 and 2010.

Dairon surviving so many attempts on his life underscored how hard it was to kill or capture one man in such a vast, primitive land. The decade-plus hunt for Osama bin Laden, who had finally been brought to justice while I was training back home for my next deployment, proved that point once and for all.

Improvised explosive devices had not been at the forefront of security threats during my first combat tour, which had initially come as a big surprise. That had all changed by the time I returned. As was true of al Qaeda in Iraq and in other parts of Afghanistan, roadside bombs had become the Taliban's weapons of choice in the five provinces in my AO. As I'm sure you've seen on television and read in other books, IEDs are hidden, lethal, and extremely frustrating to worry about. Thankfully, we had a great team of EOD (explosive ordnance disposal) experts to go on patrol with us and search for these lethal homemade bombs.

Our rules of engagement also changed while I was away. By the time I landed at Bagram in 2012, it was even harder to lay fire on a mountain ridge, as we were no longer allowed to shoot the enemy unless we were fired upon. I struggled to imagine how much harder that would have made my job as a ground fighter during my first go-around in The Stan, and felt bad for the guys that would soon be stationed at remote COPs and FOBs.

We had two Black Hawk helicopters at FOB Fenty, which was named after fallen Army Lieutenant Colonel Joseph Fenty, who was killed in 2006. The small base was filled with concrete barriers and barbed wire. Compared to spending seven months surrounded by mountains and Dairon's gang at COP Honaker-Miracle, I felt as if I were in an episode of *Lifestyles of the Rich and Famous*. I was grateful for the relative luxuries we were able to enjoy at Fenty.

Six days a week—sometimes seven in my case since I helped transport prisoners when they needed an extra body—we flew all over those five Afghan provinces for high-level meetings. Whenever the boss and Command Sergeant Major Kevin Griffin (the senior enlisted adviser to our CO) were moving, my job was to coordinate with different receiving US military units so that they knew we were coming and could track our movements. Before we visited a given area, I also had to surmise what kind of security conditions existed and what kind of military manpower was available to help me protect Colonel Mingus. At minimum, I needed fifteen soldiers from the closest base to accompany my six-man team on a given patrol. I didn't like working with any fewer than twenty-one men during the (KLE) meetings.

If we were ever shot at or encountered an IED, my men and I

would encircle our boss and the other VIPs, use our bodies as human shields, and get them the hell out of there. It was the responsibility of the other fifteen guys to engage the enemy. I guess you could say that my role was similar to that of a Secret Service agent, except I was in a war zone without the same level of protection or technology.

As you can imagine, not being able to fight back after spending seven months in Afghanistan doing just that was an extremely difficult adjustment. But this was my new job, and I was serious about doing it the right way, no matter how challenging.

My biggest test came on April 15, 2012, at Jalalabad's nearby FOB Finley-Shields, named after fallen Army Specialist James Matthew Finley and Private First Class Andrew Shields, who made the ultimate sacrifice in 2008. We had just landed at the sprawling base filled with M-ATVs and long, concrete barracks when I heard a huge crash.

The enemy had rammed a large truck into a stone wall surrounding the immense compound, where about five hundred soldiers and one thousand Defense Department civilian employees and contractors lived. A frenzied firefight began with the enemy shooting and killing a valiant Afghan soldier who was manning the base's guard tower. Seconds later, four bad guys were firing RPGs inside our base. One of them hit a fuel tank, which resulted in another jarring, deafening explosion that set some nearby wooden structures on fire.

As FOB Finley-Shields burned, my first instinct was to grab my weapon and confront the enemy. But that was no longer my role, even as our base descended into loud, fiery chaos. Colonel Mingus and CSM Griffin were by my side, and I had to get the boss as far away from the explosions and gunfire as possible.

Both men were brilliant leaders who almost certainly sensed that I wanted to run toward the commotion instead of away from it.

"Don't worry, L-T," Griffin said. "I would rather be in the mix, too, but our boys will get 'em."

Sure enough, all four insurgents were soon killed by heroic soldiers from the Missouri National Guard. As I would later find out, the counterattack was led by fearless young warriors who had just arrived in Afghanistan.

"It was one of the bravest things I ever saw in my life," Master Sergeant Joseph Schicker told the *St. Louis Post-Dispatch* after the attack. "Kids, first time in the country, charged and held [the enemy] back."

According to the paper, fourteen Missouri National Guardsmen were wounded in the firefight, which I was not initially made aware of. All of the wounded survived, and twenty-eight soldiers who fought in the battle received combat medals. The courage of these warriors not only eliminated the imminent threat posed by the four Taliban fighters, but caused many other enemy reinforcements gathered just outside the gate to retreat.

A few weeks later, FOB Finley-Shields held a ceremony honoring Alam Baik, the Afghan soldier who was killed while courageously raining down gunfire on the insurgents from the guard tower.

"I don't know why Finley-Shields was attacked, but I do know why it was defended," Lieutenant Colonel Jason Hancock said while memorializing his Afghan counterpart. "Alam Baik held the same values for his country as I do mine."

The Afghan National Army soldier's ultimate sacrifice was a stark reminder that despite all the problems I had had with the ANA during my first deployment, there were many Afghan patriots willing to lay down their lives to defeat the Taliban and al Qaeda.

Despite being on the same base on the day he died, I never got the chance to meet Alam Baik. Clearly, though, he was a hero who should be saluted by Afghans and Americans alike.

Command Sergeant Major Kevin Griffin, who had so aptly pinpointed my eagerness to fight during the Finley-Shields attack, quickly became a trusted mentor during my second deployment to Afghanistan. A former college wrestler from Wyoming, Griffin wasn't actually that big a guy, but he had a huge presence that everyone around him felt the moment he walked into a room.

Bold and confident but far from arrogant, CSM Griffin was also open and honest with every single soldier on the FOB. I don't think he was really concerned with whether people liked him, but he nevertheless cared about each of us. As soon as we met during a change of command ceremony upon his February arrival, I began to admire this tough, seasoned leader who wanted to help all of us, including me, become better soldiers and human beings. In addition to giving me combat tips, he also took an interest in teaching me how to properly manage money.

Griffin's attention to detail was unparalleled. One cold day after returning from a successful mission, the CSM's eyes were transfixed by something on the ground as our Chinook helicopter approached. As soon as we landed, I watched in astonishment as Griffin ran over to what had caught his attention: the uniform of a soldier who was walking toward FOB Fenty's chow hall.

"Why are your sleeves rolled up?" Griffin shouted at the soldier.

"My apologies, Sergeant Major," the soldier said. "I have no excuses, Sergeant Major."

Before the terrified young man could stammer anything else, Griffin had rolled down his sleeves for him.

"See? That's how it's done," Griffin said before giving him a pat on the back. "We have standards in our unit."

The young soldier's scare had ended with a sigh of relief. That's how Griffin operated: he truly wanted to make everyone around him better. The incident also earned Griffin, who had spotted the small violation from at least a football field away, a well-deserved nickname: "The Hawk."

During long talks in his office, which was inside Fenty's TOC, we bonded while talking about our respective athletic careers, even though my stories from Maryland, where I ran track, were no match for his Wyoming wrestling exploits. With a big smile on his face, Griffin told me that his future wife, Pamela, had initially noticed him on the wrestling mat while they attended the same community college before transferring to the University of Wyoming. That chance encounter led to twenty-five years of marriage and two children, Dane and Kylie.

"When are you going to start a family, Flo?" Griffin would often say with a smirk, even though he knew I wasn't married.

The command sergeant major treated me like a son, which meant a great deal when I learned that his own son, Dane, had followed in his dad's footsteps by joining the Army and serving honorably in Iraq. Incredibly, father and son had been in Iraq at the same time for a few days in 2011, and even got the opportunity to have dinner together. Griffin's eyes gleamed while telling me the story of breaking bread with his son in a war zone. After only a few minutes, I could tell that he was enormously proud of Dane.

Griffin was also extremely proud of his teenage daughter, who had just moved with her mother to Colorado from Washington state so they could be waiting at Fort Carson when their hero returned from Afghanistan. Like millions of military kids, Kylie grew up moving from base to base and school to school while not getting to spend a lot of time with her dad. Even though she missed him enormously, Kylie knew that her dad was a remarkable man on a vital mission. As the Griffin family's joke went, Kylie's father was "kind of a big deal."

Before arriving in Afghanistan, CSM Griffin had served in Operation Desert Storm, Bosnia, and three separate combat tours during the second war in Iraq, including the initial 2003 invasion. This man—whose life I was responsible for protecting as the brigade's personal security detachment commander—had done and seen more in service to his country than I could possibly imagine. Suddenly, my first seven months in Afghanistan seemed like a walk through Chicago's Grant Park compared to his six combat deployments to four different war zones.

Whenever I went into Griffin's office, he seemed to be doing research on the Afghan National Army or talking on the phone with NCOs across the five provinces in our area of operations. Afghanistan wasn't just another deployment for Griffin: he genuinely wanted the ANA—and the country—to emerge from the darkness of terrorism and war as a beacon of hope for the rest of the world.

"We are going to leave Afghanistan eventually, Flo," Griffin said one night in his office. "We have to make sure our time in this country isn't wasted, and our best chance for success is to provide the ANA with the necessary training."

When he wasn't busy doing research, Griffin talked with his family. On more than one occasion, I was sitting in his office when he would kick me out because he wanted to call Pam. Even though I had never met his wife, I could tell that she and her husband shared an unbreakable bond. It was hard for a young guy like me to imagine two people being together for that long and going through so much together; from graduating college to six Army deployments. Someday, I thought at the time, I would feel incredibly lucky to have a wife as loving and supportive as Pam Griffin.

Our boss, Colonel Mingus, was the best Army commander any soldier could hope for. Like Griffin, the colonel adored his family and led by example on and off the battlefield. A former "Mr. Minnesota" in weightlifting, he could also kick your ass in the gym despite being in his late forties.

Colonel Mingus's physical stature only enhanced the respect that every single soldier serving under his command had for their leader. That's not hyperbole, either; it would have been an honor to die while protecting Colonel Mingus or CSM Griffin. Their steady leadership and genuine care for Americans and Afghans alike represented everything that's right about the US Army and our country as a whole.

During the first six months of leading the security detail, we were shot at a few times while landing our helicopters or patrolling to and from the meetings, but never at any point did I feel that my life—or more important, the life of my boss or the other VIPs and soldiers—was in danger.

While Dairon might have been the worst enemy on my first deployment, complacency posed the biggest threat on my second. Every night, I forced myself to stay awake a few minutes longer to think about the IED blast or enemy ambush that could occur during the next day's mission. No matter how boring things got, I had to stay sharp, both mentally and physically, just as I did in my first deployment. The enemy was still lurking in the shadows, and could target my boss anywhere, anytime.

It was hard to believe that the summer was almost over when I got an email from the Army's Human Resources Command on the evening of August 7, 2012. To my complete surprise, I was scheduled to be promoted to the rank of captain following the next day's mission.

"Congratulations, Flo," CSM Griffin said when I walked into the TOC a few minutes later.

"Well deserved, Groberg," Colonel Mingus said.

After expressing my gratitude for their kind words and guidance throughout the deployment, we discussed the next day's mission, which would be to the city of Asadabad, where a high-level provincial security meeting would take place.

I had been to Kunar Province's capital city during my first deployment and several times on the second. What struck me most about the city, which is near the border with Pakistan, is that it is located right along the merging Pech and Kunar Rivers. While walking through the bustling valley, you were surrounded by two tall, imposing Hindu Kush mountain cliffs, which looked like they were staring down at you from the heavens. It was truly something to behold.

Even though my six previous visits to Asadabad had been uneventful, the rugged terrain and large population—combined with the vicious summer heat—would present serious challenges. My unit would have to bring our A game to ensure a successful meeting for the boss, who would be joined by prominent Afghan leaders.

Next, I filled out my air movement requests (AMRs) and discussed them with Sergeant Andrew Mahoney, who was responsible for deciding who would go in which helicopter and making sure everyone was ready to leave on time. Like most commanding officers, our boss hated being late, which made Mahoney's job even more critical.

After we finished planning the helicopter flights, I ran into Air Force Major Walter David Gray, a friendly Tactical Air Control Party (TACP) officer from Georgia who was half Korean and spoke with a thick Southern accent. The unlikely combination, which Gray knew most people noticed when he first met them, was the source of many self-deprecating jokes.

"Hey Flo, are y'all still going to Asadabad tomorrow?" Gray said with his usual grin.

"Yes, sir," I said while shaking the major's hand since I hadn't seen him in a while. "Will you join us on this one?"

"Actually, that's what I wanted to ask you," Gray said. "I'd also like you to meet Tom Kennedy . . . he just got here a few weeks ago.

"If it's okay with you, Tom and I would love to jump on tomorrow's mission so we can listen and learn more about the security situation in Kunar," Gray continued. "A bunch of Tom's men are also on FOB Joyce, and he'd like to meet them face-to-face. Do you think you could get us two spots on the Black Hawks?"

"Absolutely, sir," I said. "Consider it done. Please be on the flight deck by 0900.

"Nice to meet you, sir," I said as I shook Major Kennedy's hand and headed back inside the TOC.

"Likewise, Flo," Kennedy said. "See you tomorrow at 0900."

After reworking the next day's AMRs with Sergeant Mahoney, who found two spots for Majors Gray and Kennedy, I decided to head back to my room to watch *Rambo* (again) before getting some sleep. Just as I was walking out of the building, I ran into Gray for a second time. Within a few seconds, we were chatting about our time in Afghanistan and our lives back home.

"Finish strong" was David Gray's motto. Whenever things got dicey in Afghanistan, he would repeat those words.

David had first said "Finish strong" to his wife, Heather, during a 5K race they were running together, but in subsequent years, the words also motivated and inspired the soldiers he served alongside.

The major was also living proof that a human being can finish strong. That's because seven years earlier, David almost drowned during an Air Force training accident in Texas.

After he was frantically dragged out of a Laughlin Air Force Base pool on that awful 2005 day, doctors informed Heather that he was on life support. As medical experts struggled to detect activity in David's brain, Heather was told that a full recovery wasn't just un-likely; it was virtually impossible.

Heather, who shared her husband's deep faith in God, opened her husband's Bible on the Life Flight helicopter bound for Wil-ford Hall Hospital at Lackland Air Force Base in San Antonio shortly after receiving the terrible news. Through tears, she was struck by a verse: "Rejoice in the Lord always. I will say it again: Rejoice! Let your gentleness be known to all for the Lord is near" (Philippians 4:4).

How can I rejoice? Heather asked herself as her thirty-one-year-old husband lay on his deathbed with paramedics working frantically to keep him alive. Shortly after her momentary lapse of hope, Heather collected her thoughts and calmly asked God to grant her the ability always to rejoice, despite the circumstances.

At a prayer vigil later that night for family and friends who had flown in from around the country, David's squadron commander pulled Heather aside.

"All day long there has been a prayer verse in the Bible that has been coming to my mind," he said. "Rejoice in the Lord always. I will say it again: Rejoice!"

Heather's knees nearly buckled. She had told no one about the Bible verse she had read a few hours earlier. Convinced that the matching verses were no coincidence, there was no doubt in her mind that God had heard her prayer.

A few days later, Heather was at David's side when he suddenly awoke from his coma. When he eventually made the full recovery that doctors had deemed impossible, the couple was sure that they had been blessed with a miracle.

David and Heather made the most of those next seven years. They raised their daughter Nyah, then welcomed a son, Garrett, and another daughter Ava. Thanks to a startling work ethic that we would eventually witness up close in Afghanistan, David was simultaneously on his way to becoming the second-highest-ranking Tactical Air Control Party officer in the entire Air Force.

David's role as a TACP officer was to work with Army units like ours to call in and coordinate air strikes on the front lines. Before becoming a respected Air Force officer, David had served as an enlisted airman, then attended Charleston Southern University and was commissioned as an officer in 2001. Therefore, he had no trouble relating to both officers and enlisted service members during high-pressure situations on the battlefield, which quickly endeared him to everyone in our unit.

David was also a quiet but very funny guy, starting with the aforementioned fact that he spoke with a thick Southern accent despite being half Korean. Whenever he met someone new and sensed that they were surprised by the way he talked, David would crack a joke.

"Not what you thought, huh?" he would often say with his movie star smile.

In addition to his role with our unit, David was responsible for the lives of two dozen deployed airmen. While appropriately playing the role of a boss and military leader, David would also use his modest persona to play practical jokes, like the time he sternly ordered all of his airmen to assemble for an important nighttime meeting.

Instead of lecturing the nervous airmen about something they had done wrong, David had made popcorn and set up a big screen TV so that they could relax and watch a movie. By all accounts, Major Gray was just as beloved by his Air Force unit as he was by us Army guys.

David was also in remarkable shape and challenged everyone around him to perform at the highest possible level, whether inside the gym or out on patrol. His physical training exploits became so well known that he earned the affectionate nickname of "PT Ninja."

At the same time, David was the model warrior, husband, father, and Christian who was steadfast in his belief that he was living on borrowed time. At the end of a day, he would rush into his room to Skype or FaceTime with Heather and their three kids. After hanging up, David would close his eyes and say the same prayer he had been saying since the night before leaving for Afghanistan.

"Please help me keep my men safe tomorrow," he asked God.

As we reached the midway point of our deployment, the leadership, humility, and humor displayed by warriors like Major David Gray, Command Sergeant Major Kevin Griffin, and Colonel James Mingus motivated everyone around them—including me—to keep working hard. With a big mission the next day and our deployment entering its final months, we were determined to finish strong.

7 THE LAST SPRINT

I woke up at 0600 on August 8, 2012, feeling as good as any soldier deployed to Afghanistan could feel after just finding out that he was being promoted to captain. Six months into my second combat tour, it was humbling to know that my Army bosses, whom I looked up to and respected, believed that I was worthy of a higher rank.

As I got out of bed, I looked forward to officially receiving the silver captain's bars that evening. But first I had to complete the day's mission, which was to escort that large group of US and Afghan VIPs to the security meeting.

During the morning's pre-combat inspections, one of my men impatiently complained that "nothing is going to happen today."

"Complacency kills," I muttered, to remind him of the saying that had been drilled into my head since Ranger School. It was my job as an officer to keep everyone ready, including myself. Yes, we had completed six similar missions without incident, but like betting on roulette, the wheel's previous six spins are meaningless while trying to guess where the ball will land next.

As usual, the Kunar Province security meeting in the eastern Afghanistan city of Asadabad started at 1000, which meant our two helicopters needed to leave Jalalabad for FOB Fiaz in Asadabad at

0900. We would be escorting a heavy package of VIPs on this day, as three battalion commanders, two brigade commanders, two sergeant majors, and an Afghan National Army general would all be in attendance. The highest-ranking US military officer attending the meeting would be my boss, Colonel James Mingus, whom I was responsible for protecting at any cost.

The day started like any other: I brushed my teeth, took a shower, got dressed, and put on the same Army boots that I had worn since trudging through the mountains during Ranger School. Then I caught up on emails, grabbed some coffee, and checked in at the TOC for a weather report. Temperatures would be well over 100 degrees, I learned, but at least the skies would be clear. That meant as soon as the boss was ready to leave, which would almost certainly be right at 0900, we would be on our way to FOB Fiaz.

When I checked with Sergeant Mahoney, who was busy coordinating our helicopter movements while also preparing to play an integral role on the ground, he said that both choppers were ready to go.

Along with the senior military leaders, we would also be joined by a State Department diplomat and a forty-three-year-old USAID foreign service officer, Ragaei Abdelfattah.

A married Egyptian immigrant who grew to love our country, Ragaei was willing to risk his life in the mountains of Afghanistan without being able to carry a weapon since he was a government civilian. An architect who had worked for the United Nations in Egypt and the Maryland–National Capital Park and Planning Commission in the United States, Ragaei joined USAID in 2011 because he wanted to help the disadvantaged. He volunteered to spend a year in one of the most desperate—and dangerous—places in the world because he was a bona fide humanitarian.

For the past few months, Ragaei had been working in Nangarhar Province to bring electricity to the Afghan people. Additionally, he was helping the country's chronically poor farming community. Ragaei was also involved in planning the construction of new schools for Afghan girls, which I particularly admired after the special Andersille All-Girls School visit during my first deployment. Anything we could do to help improve lives for Afghanistan's desperate children had my full and unconditional support.

Even though I didn't know Ragaei very well, I was struck by his warm, unselfish nature, He was willing to die for the United States and the people of Afghanistan, which made him every bit as brave as the American service members he walked alongside.

The two officers who volunteered to join our mission the night before—Air Force Major David Gray and Army Major Thomas Kennedy—had never flown with us before. Regarding my preparation procedures, the only thing separating August 8 from any other day was making sure that these two officers knew where to meet us.

Major Kennedy, as I learned when we met the night before,

had been in Afghanistan for less than two weeks. Tom, thirty-five, had joined his unit at the midway point of its overseas tour, which presented a challenge similar to the one I faced during my first deployment. Unlike me, though, Tom was already an elite soldier with two previous deployments to Iraq under his belt, which included spending a full year in combat during the initial invasion. Without question, Tom was a proven leader who cherished the opportunity to serve.

The only thing Tom loved more than the Army was his family. As the son of an NYPD detective, Tom grew up playing hockey with his two brothers, John and George, in a New York City suburb. That eventually led him to West Point, where he excelled as a tough defenseman on Army's hockey team. After he graduated in 2000 and was commissioned as an officer, the 9/11 terrorist attack on Tom's city reinforced his desire to continue serving his country in uniform.

When Tom's oldest brother got married in Atlanta, Tom met his future wife, Kami, at the wedding. After Tom and Kami wed in 2008, they were blessed with twins: a boy, Brody, and a girl, Margaret. They were two years old when Tom kissed his beloved twins goodbye and headed to war for the first time in six years.

Before he left Fort Carson, a neighbor reminded Tom that he didn't have to volunteer for a tour in Afghanistan. Tom, who was as humble as he was polite, had a simple, poignant response.

"I'm a soldier," he said. "This is what I do."

Instead of staying home to play with his twins or cheer on his New York Rangers, as he could have, Tom poured himself into helping Americans and Afghans alike. As if we were his own kids, Tom devoted every ounce of energy to making us better soldiers.

With an impressive list of accomplishments that also included a master's degree from Columbia University, "TK," as he was nicknamed, would command the respect of everyone in the unit and, in particular, the younger guys like me. It wasn't just because of his résumé, though. Tom, a strong, blond-haired warrior who was always smiling, genuinely cared for every single soldier, regardless of rank.

It was also his dream to work for Colonel Mingus, which meant that Tom spent every waking moment getting up to speed on his new role. When I first saw TK, I could tell how proud he was to be serving the boss and his country as part of our unit.

Before leaving home, one of the last things Tom did was give each of his twins a Build-A-Bear that they had meticulously and lovingly assembled at an in-store workshop at the local mall. After hugging their respective bears before going to sleep each night, Brody and Margaret were reminded of how much their father loved them.

"Daddy flew all the way across the ocean to do something really important," Kami would tell her young twins. "He misses you so much."

My sacrifices paled in comparison to those of an American warrior like Major Tom Kennedy. Nobody back home was depending on me, and if I had had a wife and two young children like Tom, I'm not sure if I would have had the guts to deploy. What Tom, Kami, Brody, and Margaret were going through as he served in Afghanistan embodied what thousands of incredible military families put on the line every day.

As I did before every helicopter mission, I waited for Colonel Mingus and walked behind him toward the second of our two choppers. I would ride with the boss, while Command Sergeant Major Griffin would be joined on the first bird by several of my men, including Sergeant Andrew Mahoney, Sergeant First Class Brian Brink, and our medic, Specialist Daniel Balderrama.

Shortly before the twenty-minute flight to FOB Fiaz, I was told that there could be a storm on the horizon. That was no surprise, and no cause for postponement, as strong thunderstorms were common on hot summer days in Afghanistan.

But my comfort level with the mission changed once we landed at FOB Fiaz. Upon disembarking, I was told that the usual fifteen-man team of soldiers assigned to guard our perimeter would not be joining us for the one-thousand-meter patrol to the governor's compound, even though I had called and put in a request the night before.

This is not good. Upon receiving the bad news, I shook my head in disagreement even though I knew there was nothing I could do about a decision that had been made by a different unit.

Instead of fifteen perimeter guards, we would have just two additional US soldiers and an American contractor (whom I had never met) to engage the enemy if our patrol came under attack, as well as five ANA soldiers. This security element was absolutely critical for one reason: on this deployment, my unit was designed to *protect* instead of *fight*.

While outside the wire, we always maneuvered in a diamond-shaped patrol, with Colonel Mingus, CSM Griffin, and other VIPs in the middle. If we were attacked, our job was to collapse the diamond, swarm the VIPs, and bring them to safety while the designated perimeter team fought the bad guys. Without that team, I was like a quarterback going into a big game without an offensive line.

"I don't like this," SFC Brink whispered in my ear.

"Me neither," I said. "I am going to need you to take point."

It was time to be a good officer and take charge, because with the boss watching, I had to change our entire security plan in a matter of seconds.

At point, Brink would be at the very top of the formation, about ten feet in front of the diamond's tip, which is where I would be standing. I also told the five ANA soldiers joining us to go with him. While I had no reason to suspect that these Afghans were anything but patriots, the threat of "green on blue" attacks by ANA soldiers on Americans was increasing in the summer of 2012, which left room for doubt in the back of my mind. It was the last thing I had time to worry about while reconfiguring the patrol, so I moved them where my soldiers and I would be able to see them.

I was usually in the patrol's diamond, but without much of a security team to fend off the enemy, I had to move to the tip of the spear. To secure the back of the diamond, I tapped Private First Class Eric Ochart. He was the youngest member of our team, but also a well-built soldier with good instincts. If we came under attack, I knew that PFC Ochart was strong enough to do the job.

"Look, if we get hit, I need you to grab the boss and take him to safety," I said. "Use all the strength you have.

"I don't care what the colonel says; at that point he's no longer the brigade commander," I continued as Ochart nodded. "You are the boss."

"Roger that, sir," Ochart said.

I then walked toward CSM Griffin and asked him to please join Colonel Mingus and the other VIPs in the center of the diamond. He looked at me like I was crazy.

"Look, L-T," he began, even though both of us knew that I was being promoted to captain. *"I'm staying back here."*

"But Sergeant Major . . ," I stammered

"We need more rear security," he continued without pausing. "I have a rifle, and I've been doing this a long time."

I had a great deal of respect for Griffin. He was right; he had the experience to excel under pressure. I had faith in Ochart, but it gave me even greater solace knowing that a seasoned leader would also be watching from my usual rear position, which was a risky assignment.

True to form, the command sergeant major volunteered to face danger, even though he didn't have to.

"Roger that," I said. "You've got rear security, Sergeant Major."

The heat had increased—literally and figuratively—as we started the thousand-meter journey through Asadabad. Even though we had encountered nothing of note during previous patrols in the city, without our perimeter team I felt a real sense of tension in the scorching air. There was already so much to worry about when we walked through an Afghan slum, from Taliban fighters and al Qaeda terrorists disguised as civilians to the Afghan National Army soldiers themselves.

"One ANA up front has his finger on the trigger," Private First Class Ben Secor told SFC Brink.

"Keep an eye on him," Brink said. "Keep your head on a swivel."

For the first five hundred meters from FOB Fiaz to the governor's compound, the slum was on our right with the Pech River on our left. Then the road curved right into a straightaway, with a bridge we had to cross three hundred meters in the distance. The bridge was about fifty meters long. After walking another hundred meters or so, we would arrive at a set of stairs, which would lead us up to the compound.

In the beginning, everything we observed was normal. While looking toward the always raging river, we saw the same three abandoned cars that were parked on the left side of the road during our last patrol. We still checked each car, of course, but after finding nothing, we kept walking.

Despite the absence of the fifteen perimeter soldiers who were supposed to guard our patrol, the thousand-meter journey progressed quietly as our group of twenty-eight Americans and Afghans, including US and ANA officers, enlisted soldiers, a contractor, and two foreign service officers, moved slowly toward the security meeting.

About three hundred meters later, just before we reached a natural choke point at the bridge, things started to change. Inside our headsets, several of us picked up a low-level signal of what sounded like a car's engine.

"I've got a white Toyota Corolla on my ass back here," Ochart said just moments later over the radio.

Oh no.

"Do what you have to do," Brink immediately replied. "Get him off your ass."

By the time Brink finished giving his order, the suspicious white car had turned right and sped away as we stared back with our rifles raised. It was either a simple case of a frustrated Afghan driver trying to get around us or the Toyota was what we referred to as a "pusher" car, which would have shoved us right into a kill zone had Ochart not interrupted the driver.

Seconds later, our headsets once again filled with sounds of a revving engine, except that this time it was much louder. We were hearing two motorcycles bound straight toward us—at full speed—from across the bridge.

"STOP!" one of the ANA soldiers closest in front of me yelled in Pashto.

As if to obey the order, the two men jumped off their motorcycles, left them on the bridge, ran forward and then to their right (our left) toward a nearby housing complex. A few ANA soldiers started chasing them as our rifles were once again raised. All of this unfolded in a matter of seconds.

Then, moments later, Brink turned around and looked in my direction as sweat dripped from our brows. As soon as our eyes met, I knew that something was seriously wrong. There was stark silence as I realized that Brink was looking over my shoulder at something—or someone—behind me.

My head whipped around before Brink could fully raise his weapon at what I quickly realized was a man walking backward and parallel to our patrol. He was wearing black "man-jammies"—traditional garb sported by many young Afghan men—and had stumbled out of a building to our left as if he was drunk.

What the hell? Why is he walking backward?

At first glance, I couldn't figure out if this guy was a threat or an innocent, perhaps mentally challenged civilian. The only thing I knew for sure is that there was absolutely no way he was getting anywhere close to the boss.

Just then, the suspect abruptly turned all the way around. Then, in what seemed like the blink of an eye, he turned again, and was now walking rapidly toward our formation.

Without the usual security perimeter, I had no choice but to leave my post and confront him. For every split second that I wasted, he would get closer to the center of our diamond.

"Hey!" I shouted as I launched into a sprint, much like during my college track days at Maryland.

Each of the eight seconds it took to reach him felt like a silent eternity.

The man was young—nineteen or twenty at most—and he looked hypnotized or even possessed. His glassy eyes were transfixed on my boss and his face was devoid of any expression. No further doubts remained: this guy was now an imminent threat.

"What the hell are you doing?" I screamed.

There was total silence. For just a moment, the world was made up of only this devil-like figure and me. Unlike the biblical devil, however, this devil had nothing to say. He never even looked me in the eyes. Even when my face was just inches from his, the young man always looked past me—through me—as though I was not there. It then occurred to me that this man must be intoxicated.

About one second after reaching the threat, I grabbed my rifle with both hands and slammed it into his chest. Once again: nothing. His face did not change, and perhaps most eerily, he didn't make a single sound.

With the situation becoming increasingly dire, I placed my hands on his chest to begin driving the young man back. But my hands landed on a bulky package, which I instantly realized was a vest. All of my training and instincts led me to reach the logical conclusion: a bomb was attached to this young man's body.

Upon this realization, time truly stood still as my heart and my mind reached a silent accord. I was going to die.

By this point, Brink, who was watching the lethal scenario unfold so fast that he didn't have time to warn me, realized that the suicide bomber had attached a fake right hand to the outside of his man-jammies. The prosthetic hand veiled the fact that the terrorist's right arm was tucked inside his garments, with his right thumb already pressing a "dead man's trigger." All he had to do was release the button and it would all be over.

But I had to complete the job I had been trained to do: from Basic Training and Ranger School to the first time my boots touched Afghan soil. There was no time left for thinking, as only actions would make a difference now.

In my final moments, using every ounce of strength that I had, I grabbed hold of the suicide bomber's vest, and while chest to chest, started pushing the suspect away from the formation. No matter what, I would not stop until he was away from my fellow soldiers and our Afghan counterparts.

None of this was like the war scenes you've seen in the movies. During the commotion, I heard nothing. The terrorist was not shouting or chanting any prayers as he prepared to release the trigger. When I realized that the suicide bomber still had not detonated his vest as I continued pushing, I decided to grab him, turn him around, and try to throw him as far as I could. If he blew himself up with his chest falling forward and away from the VIPs, I thought, that might be just enough to protect Colonel Mingus, CSM Griffin, and the others.

After I made my final push and let go, Sergeant Mahoney, who had boldly left the formation and run in my direction, reached the suicide bomber and pushed him downward. In slow motion, I saw the terrorist land at my feet. This time, death had almost certainly arrived.

Everything went black as the suicide bomber's vest detonated, causing a massive cloud of fire and dust. But as the thundering explosion shook the entire city, I heard and felt nothing. My body flew into the air.

To this day, I do not know exactly how long it took me to wake up, but when I did, I was on the bridge, probably fifteen or twenty meters away from where the bomb had exploded. But in my first moments after coming back to consciousness, I did not know where I was. My ears were ringing while my eyes stung with dirt.

I awoke slightly propped up, my upper body reclining on my backpack, which was still strapped on. Almost immediately, I was struck by a nauseating stench of gunpowder, charred flesh, and burning hair that quickly overcame my senses.

The first color I remember seeing through the thick smoke was red, as blood was everywhere. Not yet understanding whose blood I was seeing, I quickly ran my hands over my chest, stomach, and below to make sure that everything—especially my manhood—was intact.

My assessment was that I had no internal wounds but as my eyes drifted downward, I saw a huge bone—the fibula—sticking out of my left leg. Half my calf was gone and my foot sat unnaturally askew.

I did not panic, mostly because I was confused, in shock, and felt no pain. All I did was scream a profanity and take off my helmet, which I promptly threw over the side of the bridge in disgust.

It was almost impossible to see through the smoke, and all I could hear beyond the ringing in my head was some yelling in the distance. To my relief, the shouts were in English, which meant that at least some—and hopefully, all—of my teammates had survived. Still, I knew that a suicide bombing on a US military patrol was usually part of a larger attack that involved simultaneous explosions or small arms fire.

With this reality in the forefront of my mind, I pulled my nine millimeter pistol out of its bloody holster. I cocked it and made sure that a round was in the chamber.

I was a sitting duck, and I *had* to get off the bridge before the Taliban finished me off. With blood gushing out of my shattered, melting leg, I used both hands to begin dragging myself off the bridge and toward the sounds of my battlefield brothers.

Seemingly out of nowhere, Brink jumped through the haze.

"We've got to get you out of here, sir!" he said as I looked up at his dust-covered, battle-scarred face.

Before I could respond, Brink was grasping my armor plate and pulling me away from the kill zone. A bloody trail followed us as my trusted sergeant dragged me to safety, which was a ditch where our medic, SPC Balderrama—who had a badly injured knee of his own—was waiting.

"Fix him!" Brink yelled as he took off running back toward the kill zone in an effort to save more lives.

When the dust settled a few seconds later, the utter destruction of my leg began to dawn on me. I feared the pain I knew I was going to soon feel.

"Save my leg, Doc," I gasped in desperation.

As I lay bleeding to death on the battlefield, I knew from training that I needed a tourniquet—and quickly. With the help of an Afghan interpreter who was shaking so badly that I had to assist him with opening the first-aid package, Balderrama tied on the tourniquet and—at least for the moment—got my bleeding under control.

"Water," I said while shaking my head back and forth. "Doc, I need some water."

"Negative, sir," he said. "You're going to have surgery, and you can't have any extra water in your system."

As my throat dried up, my attention turned back to my mission, and whether I had succeeded or failed.

"Where are the two principals?" I said, referring to Colonel Mingus and CSM Griffin. "Give me a status report."

Just as Balderrama was about to answer, another medic, who had just jumped down in the ditch, interrupted us.

"What is your name?" he shouted.

"Flo Groberg," I said.

"Where are you?" he said.

"Fucking Afghanistan!" I shouted as my frustration became overwhelming.

"What day is it?" he said.

"Wednes—" I started to say before cutting myself off.

"I want to know the status of the boss and the command sergeant major," I continued. "And I want to know right now."

"The boss is good, sir . . . just a concussion," Balderrama said. "The command sergeant major didn't make it."

What? Did he just say what I thought he said?

At first, the devastating news of CSM Kevin Griffin's death didn't fully register in my rattled brain. As the medics began moving me upward, the only thing I knew for sure is that I wanted to leave that ditch without giving the enemy the satisfaction of watching me being dragged out.

"Stop," I told the medics. "Put me on my feet, grab hold of my arms, and I'll hop on one foot."

"Roger that, sir," both medics said in unison.

I had hopped about twenty meters when we saw two M-ATVs, like the ones I had ridden in during my first deployment. The vehicles were based at nearby FOB Wright and weren't on our original patrol. I realized now that I had been unconscious even longer than I thought.

The medics told me one of the vehicles would take me to the base, so we kept moving in that direction until something I saw through the dust stopped me in my tracks.

Four dead bodies—Kevin Griffin, David Gray, Tom Kennedy, and Ragaei Abdelfattah—lay in a circular formation at the location of the explosion. Right away, I knew who they were, and the unforgettable sight caused my right leg—my good leg—to completely buckle. As the medics struggled to keep me upright, I hung my head while trying to come to grips with an incomprehensible tragedy.

For the first time since the blast, I was in overwhelming pain. Not the physical kind, which would arrive in a few minutes, but from an emotional shock wave that I had never felt before. As intense confusion and grief set in, my foggy mind was unable to process how these four men—all of whom were further from the suicide bomber than me—had lost their lives while mine had been spared.

Four of the last valiant words that CSM Griffin had spoken to me—"*I'm staying back here*"—echoed in my head as the medics began leading me away from the tragic site. Griffin's statement represented the truth for all four of the men who had just made the ultimate sacrifice for our country. In every sense of the word, they were selfless.

As I made my way to the M-ATV, the photos of the command sergeant major's wife and children, which I had seen countless times in his office, flashed through my racing mind. Tears began to well in my dust-filled eyes as I thought about his family. The Grays, Kennedys, and Abdelfattahs were also about to receive the worst possible news: they and the Griffins were America's newest Gold Star families. *How would I ever face them?* I was the soldier who organized this patrol, and now four tremendous men were no longer with us.

Just then I heard a lot of chatter. To my disbelief, I looked over to see a group of locals standing over the explosion site. After squinting, I realized that there was a young man, probably around the same age as the suicide bomber, who was smiling. It was a wide-eyed, sickening grin that I will never forget.

Amid the most potent mix of fury, devastation, and sadness that I had ever experienced, my emotions culminated in a moment of unprecedented, unbridled rage. There we were in Afghanistan fighting, bleeding, and dying to give these people a chance at a better future, yet as my friends lay dead, this vile human being in front of me began to laugh.

My pistol was still in the white-knuckle grip of my right hand. I raised it and aimed at his head.

Just as I thought about squeezing the trigger, PFC Ochart grabbed my arm and pulled it down.

"It's not worth it, sir," Ochart said.

"Your war is over," Brink added.

I will always be grateful to Ochart for saving another life that day.

August 8, 2012, was my first day as a captain in the United States Army and my last as a soldier in Afghanistan. It was also the worst day of my life.

8 FREAK ON A LEASH

I woke up two days later in a daze that's difficult to describe.

At first, I thought I was still on the battlefield because of all the harrowing sights and sounds still swirling through my head. In one moment, I would hear Brink and Ochart talking on the radio about the white Toyota Corolla lurking behind us in Asadabad. The next, I would picture my four fallen brothers lying in a circular formation. These voices and images—mixed with powerful painkillers and unfamiliar surroundings—left me in a wholly confused state.

It felt like tubes were attached to every inch of my body and I couldn't move. Then I imagined that I was seeing some guy with dark dreadlocks, dozens of tattoos, and a patchy beard standing directly above me and looking straight into my eyes. I ignored him for a moment while trying to figure out where I was.

As the spinning in my head slowed down ever so slightly, I remembered being loaded on a bus and packed in like a sardine with many other wounded men before falling asleep. We were heading for a Boeing C-17 that I knew would take us out of Afghanistan, but for the life of me, I couldn't figure out where we had landed. Was I in Germany—where almost all soldiers wounded in Afghanistan or Iraq were taken before heading home—or was I already in a stateside military hospital?

Once again, my racing mind was interrupted by what seemed to be a person staring down at me. Suddenly, the hazy, long-haired figure spoke.

"Hey man," he said in a familiar voice. "We're so proud of you."

Suddenly, my eyes stopped moving and met his. *Hold on, is that who I think it is? No, it can't be.*

I recognized the man's face. He didn't look like a doctor or nurse, but exactly like Jonathan Davis, the lead singer of Korn, the alternative, heavy-metal-type band that I'd been listening to since high school. Even in Afghanistan, I would listen to head-pounding songs like Korn's "Freak on a Leash" to get fired up and focused before a mission.

I started to smirk through the mask that was helping me breathe when I realized that I had to be hallucinating, much like the night I saw Mickey Mouse running next to me at Ranger School. *Why the hell would the lead singer of one of my favorite bands be in my hospital room?*

Just as I started drifting back to sleep, the man spoke again.

"What they told me you did over there was incredible," he said. "You saved a lot of lives."

As soon as my eyes reopened, I asked him where I was.

"You're at Landstuhl [Regional Medical Center] in Germany," he said. "The doctors and nurses here are taking good care of you."

His explanation made sense, which caused me to ponder the possibility that I wasn't hallucinating after all. My eyes narrowed as I took another look at the guy's face.

"Wait a second," I said. "You look like the dude from Korn."

"You're right, bro," he said with a chuckle. "I'm Jonathan Davis."

Still not completely sure whether I was dreaming, I asked him why an American rock star was visiting me at an overseas military hospital. He said that Korn was on a USO tour to entertain American troops stationed abroad.

After a five-minute conversation, I realized that the lead singer of Korn really was in my room. In addition to being an unlikely co-incidence, I was greatly appreciative for Davis's visit.

"Take care, Flo," Davis said upon leaving my room. "We'll be rooting for you."

"Thank you for coming," I said as loudly as my weak voice could manage.

What I didn't know at the time was that Davis's paternal grand-father, who served in World War II, had lost a leg while fighting in Germany, the very country where we had just met. His mother's fa-ther fought in the Pacific and miraculously survived the infamous Bataan Death March, which resulted in the tragic deaths of hundreds of American troops and thousands of Filipinos.

While Davis might have been an intense performer and an ec-centric celebrity, the heroism and postwar struggles of his grandfa-thers had made him a genuine supporter of our nation's troops and veterans. Amid my confusion and throbbing pain, Korn's lead singer managed to put a smile on my face.

After spending the next minute or two thinking about how I couldn't wait to tell my friends about meeting Jonathan Davis, my thoughts returned to the friends I had just lost on the battlefield. The pain—both emotional and physical—was overwhelming. At the same time, I was still trying to piece together how I ended up in Germany.

Then my senses suddenly became overwhelmed by terrible smells of blood and burning flesh. Within seconds, my mind wan-dered back to the chaotic aftermath of the explosion two days earlier.

Never in my life had I felt so much pain as I unleashed a blood-curdling scream in the back of an Army M-ATV in Asadabad, Af-ghanistan. There were two separate backseats in the truck, which was not designed for evacuating casualties. My head was on the passenger's side while my legs—one of which appeared to have a giant hole where the calf muscle was supposed to be—caused blood to pool all over the seat behind the driver.

Luckily, the two soldiers responsible for taking me out of the city—Sergeants Jensen and McCain—were outside the truck when I yelled in agony. I was in shock when they carried me into the vehicle, propped me up on the two seats, and slammed the M-ATV's huge door. Even though I was probably bleeding to death, I didn't want anyone to think I was weak, especially after four good men had just been killed and many more wounded. I was glad that they didn't hear me scream.

Jensen would be the driver, with McCain acting as the TC, or truck commander. As soon they jumped into the M-ATV, though, McCain looked at me in the backseat and reacted with disgust.

"What the hell, sir?" he said.

"What?" I said through heavy breathing as blood and sweat poured from my body.

"You're bleeding all over my truck, sir!" he said.

Even though I was in shock, I was nevertheless baffled by the soldier's comment, which I perceived as inappropriate and insensitive. As my incredulity morphed into anger, I released a tirade of profanity directed at McCain.

"Sir, you're about to go home, get fed meals, and be able to go to McDonald's," McCain continued, undeterred by my anger. "We're going to be here for the next three months smelling your blood in the back of our truck."

I couldn't have realized it at the time, but McCain was intentionally riling me up to ensure that I would stay awake.

"I don't give a shit about your truck," I yelled. "Give me water!"

"No, sir," Jensen chimed in. "They told us not to give you any water before surgery."

Flashing a peace sign as a young boy in France.
Courtesy of the author

My glory days on the University of Maryland track team.
Courtesy of the author

With my mother, Klara, and my father, Larry, at my Ranger School graduation, Fort Benning, Georgia, October 23, 2009. *Courtesy of the author*

The soldiers of 4th Platoon, Dagger Company, at FOB Wright, Asadabad, Afghanistan, during my first combat tour. *US Army*

Two Afghan warlords en route to fight the Taliban stop at a checkpoint. *US Army*

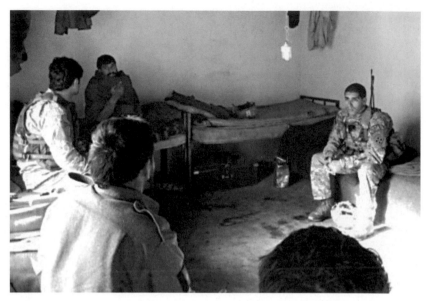

At the Afghan National Police station in the village of Shege, discussing a recent Taliban attack. *US Army*

At the Mulkhana All-Girls School, which made a tremendous impression on me. *US Army*

Saying goodbye to an Afghan friend, "Wally," near the end of my first tour in Afghanistan. *US Army*

Members of my second deployment team: (*left to right*) Clark, me, Secor, Brink, Mahoney, and Balderrama. *US Army*

Looking down on Kunar province from a UH-60 Black Hawk helicopter early in my second tour. *US Army/Staff Sergeant Alexis Ramos*

With Sergeant Andrew Mahoney. He would receive the Silver Star for his actions on August 8, 2012. *US Army/Staff Sergeant Whitney Houston*

USAID Foreign Service Officer
Ragaei Abdelfattah. *US Army*

The Gray family: Air
Force Major David
Gray and his wife,
Heather, with (*left to
right*) Garrett, Nyah,
and Ava. *Sublime Studio*

Command Sergeant Major Kevin Griffin with his wife, Pamela, and Kylie (*left*) and Dane. *Pamela Griffin*

Major Tom Kennedy, his wife, Kami, and their twins, Brody and Maggie. *Kami Kennedy*

President Barack Obama visits my hospital room at Walter Reed National Medical Center in Bethesda, MD, on September 11, 2012. My parents, Klara and Larry, and my friend Matt Sanders got to meet the president with me. I will always be grateful to the doctors and nurses who did so much to help me during the long, difficult recovery. *US Army*

Carsen, the love of my life, turns around to check on me en route to the Medal of Honor ceremony at the White House. *Lisa Orden Zarin*

Walking to the Medal of Honor ceremony in the East Room of the White House with President Obama, November 12, 2015. *US Army/Eboni L. Everson-Myart*

President Obama places the Medal of Honor around my neck. In that moment, I became a courier for my four fallen friends and their families. I will keep telling their stories to ensure that their ultimate sacrifice is always remembered. *US Army/ Eboni L. Everson-Myart*

Nyah, Ava, and Garrett Gray play Rock, Paper, Scissors with the president following the ceremony. *The White House/Pete Souza*

Reuniting with my second deployment team at the Pentagon's Hall of Heroes, November 13, 2015: (*left to right*): Ochart, Brink, me, Gen. Mingus, Mahoney, Balderrama, and Secor. *US Army/Eboni L. Everson-Myart*

Carsen and I had an opportunity to meet with former president George W. Bush and his wife, Laura, at the Wolf Trap Ball, Vienna, VA, September 18, 2016. *Courtesy of the author*

Carsen and I celebrate our December 28, 2016, engagement in front of the Capitol in Washington, D.C. *Courtesy of the author*

I had never been so thirsty in my life. My mouth was utterly dry, and I felt like without some water I would almost certainly die. The result was another steady stream of profanity; this time directed at my driver, who was just doing what he'd been told by our superiors.

The drive from the blast site to Asadabad's FOB Wright usually took about eight minutes. This one had already taken fifteen due to the many locals who had gathered to see the explosion's aftermath, as well as Afghans going about their everyday business as lunchtime approached on a busy Wednesday morning. Frustrated, I ordered Jensen to drive faster.

"Run all these trucks off the road if you have to!" I shouted.

Fortunately, the two soldiers knew that I was in no state of mind to give a serious order.

"We're going as fast as we can," Jensen said while managing to stay calm. "Hang on back there, sir."

After another five minutes or so, Jensen and McCain—who had succeeded in keeping me awake and diverting my attention from the searing pain—pulled me out of the truck headfirst. The M-ATV had arrived at FOB Wright's field hospital, where doctors and nurses who had heard about the suicide bombing were waiting outside near the flight line where helicopters would usually land. Several nurses joined the two sergeants in helping me stand up on my right leg as the blood that was still gushing from my left caused puddles to form and bubble on the hot concrete.

As soon as I stood up, I pulled a release latch on my vest that instantly disassembled my armor plate carrier. More blood splashed on the concrete as my heavy body armor fell to the ground and took me down with it. I didn't have a single ounce of strength left, and if someone didn't get me inside the field hospital soon, I was going to die.

After pulling me up and helping me get back on one foot, Jensen, McCain, and the nurses teamed up to drag me out of the brutal summer heat and into the hospital, where I finally collapsed on an operating table. After bleeding nonstop for about an hour following the explosion, I still hadn't been given a sip of water or received a single painkiller. The unrelenting combination of pain, thirst, and exhaustion was overwhelming.

Everyone on the twenty-eight-man patrol except Sergeant Brink, who was the first to spot the suicide bomber stumbling toward us, had been wounded or killed in the massive explosion. I would find out later that there had actually been *two* blasts. There was another suicide bomber that no one in our patrol had noticed at the time. As it turned out, the first explosion had caused the second bomber's vest to prematurely trigger. Other than blowing himself up, the second suicide bomber had caused minimal damage.

The hospital was already full of victims from the powerful first blast, including another high-ranking member of our patrol, Army Colonel Daniel Walrath, who was unconscious. The colonel also suffered severe injuries to his left leg and was bleeding profusely. All of us were covered in dust and had suffered wounds all over our bodies from metal ball bearings and other shrapnel. Many of us, including me, also suffered concussions and damaged eardrums.

My left pant leg and boot had already melted away, but the nurses still had to cut off what was left of my blood-soaked combat fatigues. I couldn't have cared less about that, but when a nurse took a pair of shears to my right Army boot and started putting it in a trash bag with my uniform, I almost lost my mind.

"Hey, what are you doing with that boot?" I said.

"It has to go to the incinerator since it's bloody," she said.

No way. That boot had made it all the way through Ranger School and two tours in Afghanistan, including the explosion that killed four of my brothers during my first day as a captain. I had always planned to keep my boots as a treasured memento, but now my only surviving boot had even more significance.

"That's my boot," I said while trying to lift myself up off the stretcher. "Please give it back. *Please!*"

As several nurses held me down, the supervising nurse calmly explained that she had no choice.

"It's Army protocol, Lieutenant," she said. "I'm very sorry."

I felt utterly defeated upon hearing that my boot could not be saved. As I watched a soldier quietly pick up the trash bag and take it outside, I felt like my entire US Army career would be incinerated along with it.

After a few minutes, I finally received an IV and the anesthesia that would ease my mental and physical anguish while the nurses cleaned my wounds. When I blacked out, I truly did not care about my badly damaged left leg. All I could think about was that boot, and much more important, the great men who made the ultimate sacrifice during my last day wearing it.

When I woke up a few hours later, the situation was worse than a nightmare. I was aboard a helicopter headed back to Jalalabad, with the covered body of a fallen American soldier right next me. I quickly realized that it was Command Sergeant Major Kevin Griffin.

I was too drugged up and confused to cry, but nevertheless I recognized that I was only inches away from a fellow soldier whom I had grown to deeply respect and revere. Lying next to the body of my mentor and friend was a devastating and dreadful scenario that I couldn't believe was real.

As a soldier serving in combat, impending peril often loomed. In my mind, the worst possible outcome of a suicide bombing or ambush was not losing your own life but failing to save the soldier next to you. As my eyes wandered up and down the blanket covering a true American hero, I was consumed by dejection and grief. I would have given anything to trade places with CSM Griffin, who had so bravely volunteered to put himself in harm's way.

I couldn't feel anything—literally or figuratively—by the time we landed at FOB Fenty in Jalalabad. Upon arriving at the hospital, I was thankful to see Sergeant Mahoney, who had bravely slammed into the suicide bomber after I had made my final push. He was severely wounded, particularly on his arms and hands, but had somehow survived the blast. Mahoney and I were among nine soldiers whose military careers essentially ended on August 8, 2012.

As the two soldiers closest to the first explosion, it was a miracle that we had both made it. Yet as Mahoney and I lay a few feet apart in hospital beds, I don't think either of us felt lucky, knowing that four of our brothers were dead. Distraught, I fell back asleep while experiencing a profound sense of loss.

When I woke up, every soldier from the patrol who could walk and was not in surgery was in our room to see how Mahoney and I were doing. They were joined by many other friends I had made while stationed at FOB Fenty for the past six months. While grateful to see so many friendly faces, there was someone that I wanted to speak with who wasn't in the room.

"Where is the boss?" I asked. "I want to see Colonel Mingus."

A few minutes later, in walked the colonel, who was already back on his feet after suffering a concussion. After so much misery in the hours following the attack, knowing once and for all that the boss had survived was an emotional moment.

At the same time, I was still a soldier. I wanted Colonel Mingus to know that I was ready for my next set of orders.

"Please don't let them send me home, sir," I said.

"Don't worry, Flo . . . you did your part," he said. "You're getting out of here."

That was my last memory from the short stay at FOB Fenty's hospital. By the time I saw the colonel, the drugs had *really* kicked in. The next time I was conscious, I had been flown about seventy-five miles west to Kabul, where I would be cared for at the much larger Bagram Airfield.

By this point, which I think was about twelve hours after the explosion, the blowtorch-like pain had returned. The intense burning caused me to yell at a nurse as she tried to wrap my left leg, which I was seeing for the first time in good lighting. The hole was substantial, and as I suspected, what remained of my calf muscle was a mangled mess. My left foot was also covered with blood and bruises, and riddled with metallic shards.

A few hours later, a general and several other high-ranking soldiers came into my room. After seeing how I was doing, the general approached my bed with something in his hand. Just as I began dozing back to sleep, he pinned a Purple Heart to my hospital gown.

My blackouts continued, and the next time I woke up, I was in a room with about twenty wounded service members. In addition to Purple Hearts, each of us had been given iPads connected to Wi-Fi, which allowed us to access email and Facebook.

In a somewhat comical scene, twenty guys under the influence of heavy painkillers were busy having online chats with perplexed family and friends back home. Even though I have no memory of what the heck I said during Facebook chats that day, I was able to inform several people—including Army buddies who had heard about the attack—that I had survived.

In North Carolina, where my parents had recently moved, the two most important people in my life didn't even know that I had been hit.

A few minutes later, someone handed me a cell phone.

"Call your family, Lieutenant," a soldier said.

"Mom?" I said a few moments later.

"Hey, Flo," she said in a happy tone. "How are you?"

"Okay listen, I don't want you to freak out, because I'm alive," I said. "But I got hit."

"*What?*" she screamed, shouting to my father that I had been injured.

"Mom . . . it's fine," I said while preparing to hang up. "I might lose my leg, but I'll be home in a few days . . . don't worry."

Click. My drug-induced mind prevented me from comprehending how much the news—and our conversation's abrupt conclusion—would terrify my mother, who proceeded to make about two hundred phone calls to find out where I was and what had really happened.

After spending the night at Bagram, I was put on that giant C-17 bound for Germany.

The day after my unlikely encounter with Jonathan Davis of Korn, now the third day since the explosion, I woke up to a wonderful surprise. My cousins, Anthony, Thomas, and Alexandra Stein, had made the long drive to Germany from France to see me. Even while I was hopped up on medication, their five-hour visit meant the world, and put another big smile on my face.

After a few blood transfusions later in the day, my smile began to fade when a surgeon entered my room with grim news.

"Look, I'm going to be real with you," the doctor said. "You're having surgery tonight, and when you wake up, there's a seventy-five percent chance that your left leg will be gone."

Instead of panicking, I simply shrugged my shoulders and thanked the physician for his candor. Compared to the sudden, crushing grief that had been sprung on the Griffin, Kennedy, Gray, and Abdelfattah families, the fate of my leg meant nothing.

When the doctors put me to sleep to operate that night, I was at peace with my leg being amputated. To be completely honest, I didn't care.

Surprisingly, my leg was still attached when I awoke on day four. While doctors would continue trying to save it when I got back to the United States, the likelihood of losing my leg or foot due to infection would remain high.

My next journey was to Andrews Air Force Base in Maryland, where you will often see Air Force One take off and land. During the long flight, I stayed awake long enough to start writing letters apologizing to the loved ones of those killed and wounded in Asadabad. Since I was in charge of security, I felt responsible for each death and injury. *If only my eight-second sprint could have been faster*, I thought.

When I was wheeled off the plane at Andrews, a colonel directed half the wounded service members to a bus bound for the Walter Reed National Military Medical Center in nearby Bethesda, Maryland. The other half stayed in the airplane to be flown to Brooke Army Medical Center in San Antonio.

I was told to remain on the airplane, which confused me. The colonel must have been mistaken, I thought, because he didn't seem to realize that I was supposed to be sent to Maryland, where my mom and dad were waiting.

"Sir, with all due respect, I need to be on the bus headed to Walter Reed," I told the colonel.

"Negative, Lieutenant," said the colonel.

"But sir, I am from here," I pleaded, referring to the Washington, D.C., area. "My family drove up from North Carolina and they are at the hospital."

"Son, your unit is based in Colorado," he said, referencing Fort Carson. "That means you go down to Texas."

My boss, Colonel Mingus, had stayed in Afghanistan and in fact was already back on the battlefield by the time I returned to Maryland. The other colonel wounded in the attack, Colonel Walrath, was on the same C-17 flight as me. Because such a high-ranking officer was among the wounded, the commander of the Special Operations Command, Admiral William McRaven, was there to greet Colonel Walrath as soon as we landed.

When Colonel Walrath realized that I wasn't being put on the Walter Reed bus, he asked Admiral McRaven—a universally respected military commander who planned the SEAL Team Six mission to kill Osama bin Laden—to intervene.

After talking to the other colonel, Admiral McRaven handed me a five-hundred dollar gift card that had been given to him by a military charity that assists wounded soldiers and their families.

"Give this to your parents, son," Admiral McRaven said. "Stay strong at Walter Reed."

McRaven went out of his way to ensure that my parents would be by my side during the difficult months ahead. As I began the long road to recovery at Walter Reed, it was humbling and uplifting to be on the receiving end of a kind, compassionate gesture by one of America's most distinguished military leaders.

I was formally admitted to Walter Reed's inpatient unit for wounded service members on August 13, 2012: five days after the suicide bombing. Over the next seventeen weeks, I would have twenty-seven surgeries on my left leg. Virtually every time I went under the knife, I was not sure whether my leg would still be attached when I woke up.

In those three-plus months, I never slept more than four hours at a time because doctors had to constantly wake me up and check my vitals. As soon as I was able to drift off, I was back in Asadabad.

"What the hell are you doing?" I yelled at the suicide bomber.

Every time I closed my eyes, I saw the man who killed my friends. His eyes were glassier than I remembered, and just like that terrible day in Asadabad, he wouldn't respond to my commands.

What made my frequent night terrors so scary (and frustrating) was that as they unfolded, I knew for sure that the man was a terrorist who was about to blow up himself, which had not been the case in real time. No matter what I did or said differently in my dreams, they always ended with an explosion that would wake me up in a disoriented, panicked state. Usually, I would scream "I have to stop him!" at my startled nurse.

Whenever I fell asleep, it felt like being in hell, especially when my dreams started being bombarded with grisly images of the blast scene's horrific carnage. Demons had been firmly planted in my head on August 8, 2012, which led me to ponder whether the suicide bomber really was the devil.

Between the nightmares and surgeries, my room was filled with visitors, from my parents and relatives to friends and fellow soldiers, including my buddy Saul Thompson. While I appreciated each and every visit, the daily routine became dizzying. Each morning, I also became grumpier from lack of sleep, which led my favorite nurse—Navy Ensign Haley Willis—to start limiting my visitors before noon.

Eventually, I didn't even want to sleep because of the bad dreams. Nor did I enjoy the various sleep aids and painkillers that were making me feel (and act) so strange. I was convinced that the powerful drugs were contributing to my nightmares, but even when I endured as much pain as I could to avoid the medication, I would still be back on patrol in eastern Afghanistan upon shutting my eyes.

The night terrors were the most frightening phenomenon I had ever experienced, and eventually, they spilled into my days. Soon, every moment—awake or asleep—was filled with thoughts of what I could have done to save four valiant men from returning home in flag-draped caskets.

What bothered me most was that I hadn't cried since the explosion. Even though my internal emotions had been ripped to shreds, I was still unable to show my grief on the outside. My frustrating inability to shed tears made my survivor's guilt all the more relentless. My will to live was gone.

For several weeks at Walter Reed, I was suicidal. I did not think I deserved to have made it back alive instead of Griffin, Kennedy, Gray, or Abdelfattah.

My low point arrived when a team of military investigators showed up to question me about the events of August 8. Because of opioids and the severe aftereffects of my traumatic brain injury, I couldn't recall numerous fine points about our movements or the overall sequence of events. Being questioned—and talking through the details out loud for the first time—was also an upsetting, disturbing experience.

Suddenly, my mind was once again swimming with the terrible images of August 8, including those two suspicious motorcycles, which had been intended to distract us and draw us out. I also saw the covered bodies of my fallen friends. Adding to my frustration was that even after the officials showed me satellite images of where everyone was positioned at the time of the enormous first explosion, I still failed to understand how I survived while four men standing much farther away than me had died. When my time comes, it will be the first question I ask God.

When the officials left, my mind and body felt as though they were back in shock. My depression had become insurmountable, as I shifted from nights where I chose not to sleep (to avoid night terrors) to months of physically not being able to fall asleep. I actually could have stayed awake days at a time were it not for a sleep medication that quickly became my only solace during a very dark time. Like all prescription drugs, it had side effects, the worst of which were extreme hallucinations. As you can probably imagine, persistent delusions did not help my recovery process.

With all due respect to my parents, Saul's visits probably helped the most during those very dark days. Because he had known me for so long, in and out of combat, Saul was able to sense that the demons had come, even though I didn't tell him (or anyone else) what I was feeling on the inside. Seeing the face of a friend and fellow soldier temporarily took my mind off the suicide bomber's glassy eyes, which I knew would reappear as soon as the lights went out.

On August 17, 2012, a nurse handed me a cell phone after I finished struggling to eat my breakfast. To my astonishment, Colonel Mingus was calling from Afghanistan. It meant a lot to hear from him, especially as he continued to lead soldiers on the front lines.

When he asked how I was doing, I lied and said that everything was fine. What I didn't realize was that Colonel Mingus knew Army investigators had come to see me. Even from half a world away, my boss could sense that I was less than well.

"Flo, I want you to know that this investigation is just protocol," Colonel Mingus said. "You did your job and *everyone* here is proud of you.

"I also wanted to tell you something else," he continued. "We killed twenty-seven Haqqani Network guys responsible for the attack."

Finding out that the deaths of my friends had been avenged was the best news I could have hoped for.

"Thank you so much, sir," I said to Colonel Mingus. "Please tell the guys I said hello."

When I hung up, I breathed my first sigh of relief. I think I might have even slept four hours straight.

Despite the best efforts of Walter Reed's magnificent doctors, along with Haley and two more friendly nurses named Ellen and Diamond, my leg was not healing properly. Skin graft procedures failed on two occasions, and the infections always seemed to return. No one had said it to me yet, but I started sensing that the doctors and even some nurses thought my left leg should be cut off. That was when I had the worst nightmare I can recall.

This particular dream was actually about events that had happened on August 7, 2012, the day before the attack. The dream began with me watching myself wake up at FOB Fenty in Jalalabad.

Even through narcotics, I vividly remembered my first thought of that particular day. *Should I go for a run?*

"Yes!" I shouted at my other self, who didn't react. *"Go!"*

I went on a predawn, three-mile run almost every morning in Afghanistan. For most soldiers, it was simply about going through the motions of physical training (PT), but for a former NCAA track athlete like me, running was my passion. In my dream, I watched in anguish as I decided to forgo my run that morning. Instead, I put on my Army boots for the second-to-last time and went to breakfast.

Upon waking, I realized there was a very slim chance that I would ever jog or sprint again. My decision to relinquish what turned out to be my last opportunity to go for a run would haunt me forever. It soon became one of my biggest regrets.

"What's wrong, Flo?" Haley said when I woke up in a cold sweat from my latest nightmare.

"Nothing," I said, brusquely. "Give me my backscratcher . . . these drugs make me itch like crazy."

No matter how curt I acted toward the nurses, Haley, Ellen, and Diamond were unfazed. Their calm helped me through that awful night—and so many others.

Feeling miserable from another surgery and lack of sleep, I heard a voice outside the door to my room during one November afternoon at Walter Reed.

"Hey, Captain Groberg?" the voice said. "Can I come in?"

"Whatever," I said, probably sounding like a jerk. "Yeah."

I perked up as soon as I saw the tall stranger walk in on prosthetic legs. He looked young—probably twenty-five or twenty-six at most—and he didn't have any legs *or* arms. What struck me even more, though, was how upbeat he sounded.

"What's up, Captain?" he said while extending one of his four prosthetic limbs to shake my hands. "I'm Travis Mills." He was an Army staff sergeant.

As I soon learned, Travis had stepped on an IED in southern Afghanistan on April 10, 2012, less than four months before my unit was attacked in Asadabad. Four American soldiers, including Travis, were severely wounded that day.

Travis—one of the few surviving quadruple amputees in United States military history—knew exactly what I was going through: the surgeries, the nightmares, and the survivor's guilt. Yet despite sacrificing all four limbs and experiencing his own demons, Travis had learned to do something incredible while he was at Walter Reed, where he was joined by his wife, Kelsey, and their infant daughter, Chloe. He was *smiling.*

"Look, sir, I get it," Travis said at my bedside. "I understand what you're going through . . . we've all been there.

"It sucks," he continued. "But at the same time, you *have* to stop feeling sorry for yourself."

After I told him about Griffin, Kennedy, Gray, and Abdelfattah, Travis's voice rose and his tone got even stronger.

"Open up your eyes, Captain," he said. "Those four families need you.

"It's time to get out of the darkness," Travis continued. "From this day forward, you have a responsibility to be greater than you ever thought you could be."

The fifteen minutes I was privileged to spend with Staff Sergeant

Travis Mills significantly altered my life, which was probably headed toward chronic depression or even suicide. His wounds were far more debilitating than mine, yet somehow Travis had managed to stay positive and inspire everyone around him, including his wife and young daughter.

The conversation with Travis also brought me back to the reason I originally joined the military. I did it for my country, for my family, and for my friends. I also knew the risks when I volunteered. Even when you give your very best on the battlefield, war can still steal away the lives of your brothers- and sisters-in-arms. Therefore, it was time to shut down the pity party and stop blaming myself for what had happened in Afghanistan.

I was still a soldier, but I knew that the damage to my left foot and leg was permanent and would prevent me from returning to the battlefield. It was a tough realization, but at the same time I felt lucky to have served my country while fighting alongside some of the finest individuals ever to put on a uniform. I also felt fortunate for the second chance I had been given to do better and do more.

Most important, I had the memories of four fallen heroes to honor and to live for.

In order to carry out this important responsibility, I knew that I had to make a change. Erasing all of the physical and emotional pain would be impossible, but for the first time since August 8, my negativity and denial was replaced with motivation and perseverance.

September 11, 2012, was another significant day during my time at Walter Reed. In addition to being the eleventh anniversary of the 9/11 attacks, it was the day that four American heroes—Ambassador Chris Stevens, FSO Sean Smith, and two CIA contractors, Tyrone Woods and Glen Doherty—were murdered in Benghazi, Libya.

Thirty-four days after my friends had been killed in Afghanistan, another four patriots made the ultimate sacrifice during America's long struggle against terrorism.

A special visitor was in Bethesda that day, which brought my mom, dad, and an old friend, Matt Sanders, to my room at Walter Reed. All of us were nervous, although in my case, the painkillers helped smooth out a few rough edges. But I did not know exactly what to do or say when the VIP showed up. I was excited to be meeting him, but at the same time worried that the combination of drugs and nerves would cause me to make a fool of myself.

Suddenly, a thin, athletic man wearing a crisp black suit walked through my door.

"How you doin', Flo?" he said in an enthusiastic, friendly tone.

In my room stood the fourty-fourth President of the United States, Barack Obama. I couldn't believe it.

"Wow . . . Mr. President . . ." I stammered. "What an honor to have you in my room."

"Come on now," the president said with a huge smile. "The honor is all mine."

For a split second, the room was silent. Perhaps sensing that we were nervous, the most powerful man in the world broke the ice.

"Larry!" President Obama said while extending his hand to my dad, a staunch Republican. "How are you?"

After my dad and my commander-in-chief shook hands and exchanged greetings, President Obama turned his attention to my mom, who was normally excited and extremely talkative. During this surreal encounter, however, she was speechless.

"Klara!" the president said. "You are so beautiful."

After introducing himself to my friend Matt, President Obama came to my bedside and started talking about the day that changed my life. It was immediately clear that the president had been briefed on what happened in Asadabad, and that he truly cared about my fallen friends and everyone else who had been hurt.

"What you did out there . . . I don't think this country could ever adequately repay you," President Obama said. "I am so damn proud of you."

"Thank you, Mr. President," I said.

"I wish we were meeting under better circumstances," the president continued. "But please know that you represent everything that's great about America, and everything that I love about this country."

"Serving was a great honor, sir," I said.

Somehow, the president already knew that my family had Chicago roots, which led to more smiles and a conversation about the upcoming football season, during which we would all be rooting for the same team. We profusely thanked the president after he signed a Chicago Bears T-shirt for my mom. Then he bid us farewell.

"If there is anything you ever need from me, Flo—*anything*— I am just a phone call away," President Obama said. "Here's my aide's business card."

That promise would stay with me during the many difficult days and nights to come.

"I'll never forget you," President Obama said.

The president's visit was the greatest honor of my life to that point.

Four days later, I awoke to another surprise when a White House aide showed up at my door. In his hand was a box with a signed jersey from Jay Cutler, the quarterback of the Chicago Bears. I later learned that President Obama had personally called the team and asked for the signed jersey.

With all due respect to Jay Cutler and the Bears, that jersey meant so much more to me than anything related to being a football fan. It was an affirmation of the president's vow that he would not forget me which to me signified that he would also remember my fallen and wounded teammates. Like Admiral McRaven's kindness a few weeks earlier, President Obama's thoughtful gesture truly meant the world.

After six overseas operations and many more surgeries and nightmares after coming home, I finally checked out of the hospital's in-patient unit on December 18. Getting through the most challenging seventeen weeks of my life was the first semi-decent feeling I had experienced in a while, but at the same time I knew that my journey to recovery was far from over. Because of the infections ravaging my leg and the demons that were still trapped inside my head despite my best efforts to stay positive, I would be in and out of Walter Reed for the next two and a half years.

9 A LEG UP

Being inside a Fort Carson gym in December to welcome home my unit from Afghanistan was one of my life's most consequential moments.

As soon as the returning troops were reunited with their ecstatic families, I got out of my wheelchair to applaud. One by one, the soldiers who had been at my side during that horrible day in Asadabad—Brink, Ochart, Mahoney, Balderrama, Secor, McCain, Jensen, and so many others—came by to say hello and give me a hug. I thanked each of my brothers not only for their courage on August 8, 2012, but for hunting down and killing the Haqqani Network terrorists who had ordered the attack.

Colonel Mingus had invited me to the homecoming ceremony, and seeing him for the first time since I left Afghanistan was another emotional moment. Though still reeling with my feelings of shame, regret, and guilt about losing four men, I suddenly felt enormously grateful when I saluted my boss and shook his hand. I was thankful that Colonel Mingus, who would soon become a general, had survived the harrowing attack.

After the emotional ceremony, Colonel Mingus and his wife, Amy, invited us to gather at their home near Colorado Springs. In the boss's kitchen, I took a deep breath and introduced myself to Pamela Griffin, who immediately reached out to give me a hug.

"It's wonderful to finally meet you, Flo," she said.

"Kevin had such a huge impact on my life," I told CSM Griffin's grieving wife. "Your husband meant so much to all of us."

Looking into the tearful eyes of Pam—who had lost her husband just four months earlier—was excruciating.

"I would give anything to bring him back," I said. "I am so sorry for your loss, and want you to know that the other guys and I will always be here for you."

"Thank you, Flo," Pam said through tears.

Pam Griffin inspired me the same way Heather Gray and Kami Kennedy eventually would. All three Gold Star wives, I would soon learn, are astonishingly courageous people.

Upon returning to Maryland just before Christmas, I became an outpatient at Walter Reed. Around-the-clock care had certainly helped the healing process, but my leg was still in rough shape and at constant risk of infection.

During my first few weeks as an outpatient, getting out of my new apartment in Bethesda and drinking with my high school, college, or military friends in the Washington area helped me temporarily escape the physical and emotional pain I was still experiencing. In addition, coming home with a buzz at night usually helped me fall asleep, even if it was for only a few hours. If the choice was between a morning hangover and the hallucinations I routinely experienced while taking sleeping pills, I picked the former.

Of course, this lifestyle was not healthy. It began taking its toll on my liver, not to mention my leg. It was also becoming obvious to the fine military doctors and nurses at Walter Reed that I was still struggling.

"You have to take care of yourself emotionally as well as physically, Flo," Haley said. "I know you've been through a lot, I really do, but you have to take better care of yourself."

Haley was candid with me because she knew she was my favorite nurse.

"I'm fine, Haley. Don't worry about me," I said. "I'm working on it; I just can't sleep without the IV Benadryl that I received as an inpatient. Pills are the only thing that can put me to sleep when the pain takes over."

A few days later, I came into Walter Reed with yet another infection in my left foot. Then, a few weeks after that episode, I ran into Haley at a birthday party for one of my former nurses. I must have looked exhausted.

"Flo, I have to be honest with you," she said. "I have seen you go through so much over the last seven months.

"All of your hard work to get back on your feet has been incredible," Haley continued. "But have you considered the alternative?"

Haley was pointedly staring at my PICC (peripherally inserted central catheter) line, which was driving antibiotics straight into my vein. She was implying that I consider amputation of my left leg.

"Look, I understand that limb salvage is one of the hardest medical decisions to make, but sometimes amputation can lead to a better quality of life," she said.

Despite our strong nurse-patient relationship, Haley's bluntness surprised me.

"The prosthetics are phenomenal these days," she continued. "Plus, your recovery time will be so much faster, and it could help you with the sleepless nights and the need for sleeping pills."

I paused for a moment to think about what Haley was saying. I had seen a few of my military friends elect to amputate, and they were already making major progress. Maybe Haley was right, even if I couldn't bring myself to accept it.

"I get what you're saying: this leg is awful and I know that I'll never run again," I said while looking at the ugliness beneath my bandage. "But at the end of the day, it's still my leg. I can't volunteer to amputate it."

"I understand, Flo," she said. "Just remember that you will always have that choice."

Haley's frank talk was the moment that I decided to take the difficult route and keep my leg, which would mean more pain and more drugs.

Over the next few months, I knew that I had to come up with a plan. I understood that the severity of my injuries and the decision to choose limb salvage over amputation meant that I could probably never serve as an infantryman again. That meant transitioning my military mind-set into that of a civilian, and there I was lost. For the first time in my adult life, I had no idea what my future would entail.

Transitioning into the civilian world was the hardest thing I had done since learning English as a young immigrant. So, my first mission was to find my next passion. I sat down, took out a sheet of paper, and wrote down things that I absolutely would hate to do and things that I would find rewarding.

Immediately, I wrote that I could never work a five-day-a-week, nine-to-five job in front of a computer. I had to be outdoors, able to meet with people, and part of a team that would work together to accomplish a mission. In short, I was looking for the closest thing to make me feel whole again, like the Army once did. Finding that next passion—and the support system I would need to carry out my transition to civilian life—was my biggest challenge.

Another challenge was maintaining a rigorous physical therapy schedule as part of the Wounded Training Brigade's Bravo Company at Walter Reed, which I would visit every day. Thankfully, I had a great squad leader in Army Staff Sergeant Todd Askew, who worked incredibly hard to help wounded service members keep our hectic physical therapy and appointment schedules organized.

When I first met SSG Askew, I thought he was going to be a hard-ass. But within a few conversations, I knew he was a smart, compassionate soldier who genuinely cared about my recovery.

Like all good NCOs, SSG Askew made sure that I attended physical therapy five days a week, as well as all my other appointments. I had never realized that recovery could be like a full-time job, but the Wounded Training Brigade quickly changed my thinking. In addition to frequent PT appointments, I had to see neurologists for my traumatic brain injury, dermatologists for my skin burns and rashes, gastroenterologists for my severe heartburn caused by medications, urologists—due to the blast effects—to preserve my ability to some-day father children, therapists to deal with my post-traumatic stress, and infectious disease specialists to combat infections in my leg. I guess you could say that the Wounded Training Brigade kept me busy.

Even with such an extensive medical appointment schedule, I knew that I had to set myself up for success. So I did two things that would change the course of my life: I applied to graduate school and eventually decided on attending the University of Maryland University College (UMUC). I also decided to find myself a mentor.

I knew that attending school full-time would be impossible due to my medical appointments, but UMUC allowed me to attend class remotely. I also felt comfortable with the institution because I had completed my undergraduate studies at the University of Maryland.

In the spring of 2013, I enrolled and began my pursuit of a master's degree in Management with a specialization in Intelligence Policies. I was always fascinated with the intelligence community, and figured that this might be a great opportunity to learn more about it with a potential career path in the horizon.

That same spring, my friend Rory introduced me to Jared Shepard, who is the founder of Warriors Ethos, an incredible nonprofit organization dedicated to helping veterans like me take the next step. He was also president and CEO of Intelligent Waves, a successful IT and networking company.

Jared is a veteran who brilliantly transformed himself from military sniper to IT guru after conquering the same initial fear of transition that I was experiencing. After listening to my story, Jared promised to work with me, on one condition.

"I will help you find the next mission," he said. "But I will only do that if you promise me that you will listen and put the work into it."

After assuring Jared that I was ready to go, he offered me a hand up instead of a handout. As it turned out, that was exactly what I needed. For both of us, it was a risk worth taking, so we took it. That's what infantrymen do.

Jared and his team quickly took hold of my résumé, and together we retold my story to identify the military experiences that could best translate into civilian career strengths. Next, we worked on rehearsals and mock interviews to increase my confidence and comfort level. I also learned that I needed to work on my etiquette, refrain from using chewing tobacco in the office, and cut down on my use of acronyms, all of which were bad military habits.

The Wounded Training Brigade allowed me to take part in an internship program for up to twenty hours a week. So for the first three months as a Walter Reed outpatient, I was able to spend four days a week working with Jared. During my time in his office, I watched, listened, and learned how his team communicated, dressed, and conducted themselves. In meetings, which I attended after buying new suits and dress shoes, I was a follower instead of a leader. But I was also learning more and more each day.

After three months working with Jared and his team, I finally felt ready to lead in the civilian world. That was until I woke up one morning with a burning sensation in my left leg.

Damn it.

I had experienced that feeling before, and knew it wasn't good. Immediately, I went to see Kara, who helped me with wound care at Walter Reed. It took her only a minute to conclude that I had another infection. For a moment, the frustration that I had felt during my first period in the hospital reared its ugly head.

"Just when things are starting to go well, this crap has come back," I said.

"It's all part of the process, Flo," she said. "Limb salvage is never easy."

An hour later, my left foot was red-hot and being examined by the talented Dr. Shawen, whom I had nicknamed "the magician" for all the wizardry he had performed to save my leg.

"It's definitely an infection," he told Kara. "Let's get him ready for surgery first thing in the morning."

This would be my thirty-second surgery since the blast, which had opened the door for the infectious parasites that had burrowed their way into my wound. While I was working around the clock to recover, the parasites were working just as hard to defeat my immune system.

After Dr. Shawen removed the infected tissue and cleaned out my wound during surgery, I spent another week—now my eighteenth since coming home—as a Walter Reed inpatient. The difference was that this time around I was working on graduate school papers and jumping on work-related phone calls from my hospital bed.

I was in a walking boot for a month after my release, which required frequent visits to Kara, who would check the status of my stitches. Once they were removed, it took another few weeks of careful walking and wound cleaning before I felt comfortable with the progress. From that point forward, the lasting effect of my injuries was more about annoyance than overwhelming pain. I had fallen behind at work, but because of the time management and dedication skills I had honed in the military, I was able to catch up.

During the summer of 2013, I spent six weeks at the Center for the Intrepid at Fort Sam Houston in San Antonio working with a genius prosthetist named Ryan Blanck. Ryan had invented a revolutionary brace called the the Intrepid Dynamic Exoskeletal Orthosis, or IDEO. I had lost the ability to move my left foot up and down and from right to left. This brace, which was designed to bypass the mechanics of the human ankle, did that for me.

While I knew that sprinting or running long distances was out of the question—which was still difficult to accept for someone who loved running as much as I did—the IDEO brace allowed me to walk and even jog for short periods of time. It also reduced the pain I felt while maneuvering. The only lingering problem was my skin grafts, which would make contact with the brace and occasionally open up my wounds. Despite those occasionally aggravating issues, Ryan and the IDEO brace made a monumental difference in my recovery.

That same summer, I found an opportunity with the Department of Defense, where I would begin working in the intelligence field and ultimately discover that next career passion. Working with members of the military and civilians alike, I tackled projects that made a difference and intrigued me at the same time. I was doing something that was beyond just making money; it was about doing my part to serve my country in a different way.

I was finally happy again. I had a routine with my physical and mental rehabilitation, as well as a career in front of me and a new path. Over the course of the next year, my life became routine; even boring, some might say.

My last leg surgery took place on February 14, 2014, Valentine's Day. Thanks to the love and support I received from my family, friends, fellow soldiers, doctors, nurses, and geniuses like Ryan and Jared, I would be able to take the next step in life without a cane and with my left leg still firmly attached.

A chance encounter in the fall of 2014 was the moment when I started permanently putting my life back together.

October 3, 2014, was an exciting day in Bethesda, Maryland. Both of the Beltway region's hometown baseball teams, the Washington Nationals and Baltimore Orioles, had home playoff games on that Friday afternoon. The postseason excitement, combined with the workweek's conclusion, put a buzz in the Mid-Atlantic air that was tempered only slightly by the chills of early fall.

Using the dropping evening temperatures as an excuse, I planned to sit in my apartment that night instead of going out. With chewing tobacco handy and my wounded leg covered by white bandages and gray University of Maryland sweatpants, I was playing *Call of Duty* on my Xbox, which transported me back to my days of leading soldiers in battle.

Getting the Bethesda apartment eighteen months earlier marked the first time I had lived alone since a few months prior to my second deployment. It was a major challenge at first, especially considering that my apartment was on the second floor of a walk-up, which meant that there was no elevator. Climbing stairs every day, especially when I was wearing a large protective boot, was tough. Taking a shower was one of my most difficult tasks for that first year and a half, as my left leg always had to be covered up to the knee by a plastic sheath. I called it my "leg condom."

By October, I was finally on the cusp of showering normally. Yet despite all the progress that had been made, I still had trouble sleeping. Even a year and a half after my injury, I could barely close my eyes without the dreaded sleeping pills.

That troubling trend might have continued if not for a text message that evening from my friend Marie Mimiaga, whom I had known since my freshman year of college. We hadn't talked in a while, but she knew I was back from Afghanistan and wanted to catch up.

"Come meet my friends for happy hour in D.C.," she wrote after we exchanged a few initial texts.

To be honest, I was enjoying my videogame and evening dip, and didn't really feel like dealing with a barful of rowdy Nats and O's fans, in addition to the usual Friday night revelers.

"I don't know if I can make it," I lazily replied.

"Come on, it will be fun," Marie wrote. "Plus, you should meet my friends—there will be a big group of girls."

Suddenly, Marie was making a lot of sense. Within a few minutes, I was putting on the leg condom and taking a shower before changing into some decent clothes and heading out the door.

My left leg had started to ache by the time I got off the Metro and arrived at a bar called Science Club on 19th Street. Just as I was about to walk inside, I saw a pretty girl sitting on the patio with a few friends drop her cell phone.

We reached down at the same time to retrieve the phone. I then picked it up and took a quick glance at the screen to make sure it wasn't broken before handing the phone back to her.

"Here you go," I said to the attractive, dark-haired woman with striking eyes.

"Thanks so much," she said with a smile.

As I continued into the bar to look for Marie, I started kicking myself. Why didn't I ask for the beautiful girl's name and offer to buy her a drink? *Damn it.*

I couldn't find Marie, so I decided to sit down at the only open seat I could find and rest my leg. By the time I finished my first beer, the place was packed and extremely loud, so I decided to text Marie to see if her group had gone somewhere else. To my surprise, she said everyone was hanging out at a large table upstairs.

After struggling to climb the Science Club's stairs, all I could think about was popping a painkiller, even though I could hear Haley's voice in the back of my head warning me not to mix pills with alcohol.

Just as I was about to break the rules, I stopped in my tracks. Sitting at the group's long table was the same young woman who had dropped her phone. They must have moved from the patio to the second floor while I was waiting by the bar.

This time, I refused to let the chance to introduce myself fall by the wayside.

"Hey, it's nice to see you again," I said. "I'm Flo."

"Likewise! I'm Carsen," she said with another smile. "So you know Marie?"

"Yep, we briefly ran track together my freshman year of college, but it's been years since I've seen her," I said.

The bar may have been crowded that night, but as soon as I sat at the head of the table, Carsen and I might as well have been the only two people there. We had a lot in common, including the fact that neither of us had intended to go out that night. As it turned out, Carsen had been working on an important office project when her colleagues convinced her to join them for a few drinks.

"Well, I'm glad we both decided to go out," I said.

"So am I," said Carsen.

In addition to her beauty, what made Carsen so extraordinary was that she *listened*. When she noticed that I was wearing a black bracelet, which had been given to me by my battle buddy Brink, I told her there had been a terrible suicide bombing while I was serving in

Afghanistan. The names emblazoned in silver lettering on my brace-let, I explained, belonged to my fallen brothers-in-arms.

The conversation didn't end there. Carsen asked me about each fallen hero and how their families were doing. She then inquired about my injuries and my time at Walter Reed and even my first deployment to Afghanistan. I told her about living in close quarters with my fellow soldiers in the "Wild West," where enemy fighters like Dairon spent every day trying to kill us. (I had recently been told that Dairon was killed by a Coalition air strike in 2013.)

Even though we had just met, I could tell that Carsen genuinely cared about not only my time in the military, but me as a person.

About an hour or so later, Marie floated the idea of heading to a less congested nearby restaurant, where the kitchen was open late. As everyone got up while continuing to talk and stumble around, I told Carsen that I would meet her there after a quick stop at a conve-nience store across the street. Because it had gotten so loud, I didn't really hear her reply, which I assumed was a simple "okay."

I bought some chewing tobacco and headed to the restaurant. The ache in my leg was gone without taking a single painkiller. Meet-ing Carsen, who I immediately knew was someone special, had all but erased the pain.

When I arrived at the restaurant, however, she wasn't there. As if I were on a mission in Afghanistan, I went over to Marie to ask for a status report.

"Carsen left," she said. "I think she thought you went home."

Oh no. She probably thought I was a complete jerk for leaving without saying goodbye, especially after such a lengthy conversation.

Dejected, I sat down at the table and sipped my beer. That was until Marie, who was at it again with her wonderful ideas, chimed in.

"Do you want Carsen's number?" she said.

"Yes, please!" I said while profusely thanking her.

Within seconds, I was texting an apology to Carsen along with a brief explanation for why I left. I was grateful that she understood, and after I asked if I could take her out for a more formal date, Carsen said that she was free that coming Sunday.

For the first time since moving to the United States, I did something other than watch football on a Sunday in October. Needless to say, going out with Carsen was much better. During dinner, I realized how lucky I had been to find her.

Because of Carsen's patience and willingness to listen to even my most traumatic war stories, I was soon able to get a full night's sleep without pills or alcohol. Finally, my life started to resemble something normal thanks to my remarkable doctors, nurses, squad leader, fellow wounded warriors, and most of all, my new girlfriend.

"Hello?" I said, answering a cell phone call from an unknown number.

On a hot, miserable day in September 2015, almost a year after I had met Carsen, I was on a training exercise for the Department of Defense in Nevada, when I received the call.

"Is this Captain Florent Groberg?" a male voice said.

"Yes, sir," I said, despite having medically retired from the Army a few months earlier, in July.

"This is Colonel Slaney, and I need you to listen very carefully," he said. "On Monday, September 21, between the hours of 1400 and 1430, you'll be receiving a call from a Pentagon senior high-ranking official."

I didn't know what to say.

"Is the number that I just called you on a good number for the call?" he asked.

"Roger that, sir," I replied.

"*Do not miss this call*, Captain," Colonel Slaney said with authority before saying goodbye and hanging up.

I had absolutely no idea what to make of the colonel's phone call.

More than three years after the attack in Asadabad, had investigators determined that I was partially responsible for the deaths of four men? Or, perhaps, was I about to receive some sort of recognition for confronting the suicide bomber? I was baffled.

At the Pentagon, where I had recently started working in a civilian capacity, I had heard rumors about my name being floated for the Distinguished Service Cross. I didn't feel like I deserved any award, let alone the second-highest that can be bestowed on a US Army soldier.

I didn't know whether I should alert my parents and Carsen to some potentially good news or ask them for help in finding a good lawyer.

No matter how things turned out, my hope was that the phone call would lead to some form of closure for the Griffin, Kennedy, Gray, and Abdelfattah families. As long as the forthcoming news helped ease some of their pain, I didn't care what happened to me.

When September 21 arrived, Carsen sat on the couch and watched *The Ellen DeGeneres Show* to pass the time while I stayed in the kitchen to think and work on a graduate school paper.

Then, at 1420 (2:20 p.m.), my cell phone finally rang. Like the previous call from the colonel, the screen said *Unknown*.

"Hello?" I said.

"Hi, this is the White House," a female voice on the other end of the line said. "Would you please hold for the President of the United States."

I was stunned.

The fact that the president was calling all but eliminated the possibility of the Distinguished Service Cross. By this point, all I could do was clear my throat and get ready to talk with the leader of the free world.

"Hey Flo, how are you?" said President Obama, who seemed to be picking up right where we had left off three years earlier. "I hope you've been recovering well."

"I'm doing great, Mr. President," I said. "Thanks again for coming to visit me and my family in the hospital."

"Thank *you*, Flo," he said. "Listen, I'm giving you a call to let you know that you'll be receiving the Congressional Medal of Honor in a few weeks."

I was speechless.

After explaining that the Pentagon would coordinate logistics, the president concluded our call on a gracious, humbling note.

"I am so proud of you," President Obama said. "Ever since I first heard your story, I had a feeling this [Medal of Honor] recommendation would cross my desk."

After sincerely thanking the president and saying goodbye, I was quiet. Finding out that you will receive the nation's highest military award doesn't make you want to jump for joy or open a bottle of champagne. It is a solemn moment.

The Medal of Honor, I said to myself in the kitchen, was far bigger than any one service member. In my case, it would represent four selfless men who made the ultimate sacrifice. From that day forward, their names would not only be on my wrist and in my heart, but I promised myself that they would be spoken every time someone asked to hear my story.

After taking a few moments to digest the unexpected news, I looked at Carsen, who had muted *The Ellen DeGeneres Show* while calmly waiting for my reaction on the living room couch.

"I guess our lives just changed," I said.

After a brief moment of reflection, Carsen unmuted *Ellen* and I joined her on the couch. Then, without saying anything else, I resumed working on my graduate school paper.

10 A GREATER HONOR

On November 12, 2015, I walked into the East Room of the White House shoulder to shoulder with the President of the United States. "Hail to the Chief" boomed and echoed through the hallowed hall while dozens of cameras clicked. The room was hot, bright, and packed with people, which made me immediately uncomfortable.

I was slightly reassured knowing that within the crowd of that large room were my family, friends, Army brothers, fellow Medal of Honor recipients, and most important, the loved ones of Command Sergeant Major Kevin Griffin, Major David Gray, and Major Thomas Kennedy.

All I could think about was staying in step with the president and reaching the stage without making a fool of myself. I would stand to President Obama's right, in front of a blue Medal of Honor flag, which has thirteen white stars and gold trim that was almost an exact match for the East Room's regal gold drapes.

Upon reaching the stage, I looked into the audience for the first time and became overwhelmed. When the president eventually began his remarks following an opening prayer, the ceremony would be carried live by cable news outlets and online throughout the world, including at military bases in Afghanistan.

In addition to being nervous, my left leg was starting to hurt—badly. For reasons I cannot explain, it was the worst pain I had felt in my leg and foot in more than a year.

Standing at attention in the White House, I thought about a conversation that I had had with my dad shortly after informing my parents that I would receive the Medal of Honor. We had discussed how it would reflect on the Army if an infantryman was seen sitting during a nationally televised ceremony. With my branch's pride at stake, I decided to stand even though several past Medal of Honor recipients—all tougher men than me—had elected to stay seated because of their injuries.

I soon realized that I had made a huge mistake. As soon as the Army's chief of chaplains, Major General Paul K. Hurley, began the invocation with "almighty God, we hear your words," my leg started to shake.

At the precise moment I was about to panic, a calming thought entered my mind.

Stop, Flo. Breathe. Relax. Bend your knees. It won't be long.

"Today, we remember your goodness and the sacrifice of all our soldiers," General Hurley said in prayer. "Heal our hearts with the tears of their grieving families."

Their grieving families. All three were sitting right in front of me in the row behind my parents, Carsen, and her family. As I looked into their eyes, I felt anxious, but also filled with resolve to ensure that I made it through the ceremony, where their loved ones would soon be honored by the president. This day was about them.

Without their strength, along with the support I had received from so many others during the seven-week whirlwind that followed the president's phone call, I would never have made it to the White House to begin with.

"You talked to the President of the United States on the phone?" my mom exclaimed after I called my parents to tell them that I would soon receive the Medal of Honor.

"Yes, Mom, and he actually mentioned you during the call," I said. "He said that he was looking forward to seeing you again, and that he trusted that you won't tell a soul about the ceremony until the White House makes an official announcement."

It was a white lie. President Obama had actually told me to please keep the news to myself, which meant that already I was technically violating an order from the commander-in-chief. Still, I couldn't keep something this big from my mom, who screamed with joy before I could finish explaining what the Medal of Honor signifies: millions of US troops and veterans, fallen brothers and sisters, and Gold and Blue Star families. It represents our flag and every single person who ever put on a uniform.

"I won't tell anyone, Flo," my mother said after calming down. "But you have to tell your father, too."

My dad's reaction was different from my mom's. He was stoic and almost strangely at ease, as if he knew the totally unexpected news was coming.

"I am proud of you," he said. "Now comes a big responsibility."

Just as we were about to hang up after talking for the next five minutes or so, my dad said something else.

"I also want you to know something, Flo," he said. "I love you."

My father rarely said those three words, not because he didn't care, but because our relationship had always been built on tough love. Having him say it meant a lot, and gave me the confidence I needed to proceed with the three extremely difficult conversations that came next.

As soon as I hung up with my parents, I sat down to call each Gold Star wife: Pamela Griffin, Heather Gray, and Kami Kennedy. When I dialed each phone number, I dreaded the ensuing conversation. Would these grieving women bristle at the idea of me getting an award after their husbands had died during a mission that I had planned? Even after having met each kindhearted, compassionate widow, I had no idea what to expect.

One thing was certain: while I already knew that the loved ones of USAID Foreign Service Officer Ragaei Abdelfattah were overseas and couldn't make it to the White House, I planned to forgo all ceremonial proceedings and press opportunities if Pam, Heather, or Kami declined to attend.

To my surprise, all three Gold Star widows were excited by the news. They each promised to be there, which took a tremendous amount of courage since they undoubtedly knew the day's events would be a painful reminder of how their husbands died. Their enthusiasm would always mean the world to me, and I could not have been more grateful.

In the days to come, I was told that I could bring up to one hundred people with me to the White House ceremony, which would take place the day after Veterans Day. While Carsen and I worked on the invitation list, the Army assigned me to work with a few amazing public affairs folks who prepared me for many different public speaking scenarios, including television and radio appearances.

During mock interviews, the public affairs officers (PAOs) trained me to stay away from controversial topics and to remain focused on the main message that I wanted to spread, which was honoring my living and departed Army brothers and sisters.

After three tense, busy weeks, the White House finally made its formal announcement on October 14.

On November 12, 2015, President Barack Obama will award Captain Florent A. Groberg, US Army (Ret), the Medal of Honor for conspicuous gallantry. Captain Groberg will receive the Medal of Honor for his courageous actions while serving as a Personal Security Detachment Commander for Task Force Mountain Warrior, 4th Infantry Brigade Combat Team, 4th Infantry Division during combat operations in Asadabad, Kunar Province, Afghanistan on August 8, 2012.

Captain Groberg will be the tenth living recipient to be awarded the Medal of Honor for actions in Afghanistan. He and his family will join the President at the White House to commemorate his example of selfless service.

That night I received more than two thousand text and social media messages, along with countless congratulatory phone calls and emails. Local and national news crews also set up camp outside my condo in the heart of our nation's capital, even though I was under strict orders not to speak with the media unless it was organized and monitored by the Army's PAOs.

The commotion created feelings that could not have been more conflicting. While I welcomed hearing from close friends and family, I was still ashamed to be receiving all of this attention and prominence for such a tragic incident.

When the military-sanctioned interviews began, I struggled to tell my story. The PAOs had done a great job in preparing me, but I wasn't emotionally ready to speak about the bombings over and over again, let alone in front of the media's most prominent journalists, including several from my native France.

I was dreading the week of the ceremony, which I knew would be filled with interviews and events. Even though my life had already changed to a degree, becoming a Medal of Honor recipient was quickly becoming a reality that I was still not ready to accept.

I was told to check in to the Sheraton in Arlington, Virginia, the evening of Tuesday, November 10, 2015. This would be my staging point for the next five days. But before Carsen and I went to the hotel, I had a critical task to accomplish. Carsen had recently agreed to move in with me on the condition that I repaint one wall of her old apartment when she moved out. I hate painting, but of course this trade-off was well worth a couple hours of labor.

Of all the days her lease expired, it had to be two days before I received the Medal of Honor. Alone in an empty apartment, I began a task that I thought I would loathe when I realized it was actually a cathartic exercise. Inside a literal blank canvas, all I had were my thoughts, which began to pour out.

Two hours later, I closed the door to Carsen's former apartment for the last time with a new sense of resolve. The Medal of Honor was not about me, nor would it change me as a person.

I was on edge upon arriving at the Sheraton until I saw a familiar face that instantly put me at ease. It was Sergeant First Class Korey Staley: the same soldier who had told me to "shut up and listen" during my first tour in Afghanistan. Without preaching, SFC Staley had taken me under his wing and taught me how to lead troops in combat, which eventually helped me become an effective US Army officer.

While I had invited Staley to the ceremony, I did not realize that he would be among the first people I saw. It was a big deal, especially with all the butterflies flying around in my stomach as ceremony week began. After sharing a hug, the three of us went upstairs to the living quarters (actually a luxury hotel suite) that Carsen and I would share.

That evening in Arlington, I would see all my August 8, 2012, teammates in the same room for the first time since I had flown to Fort Carson to help welcome them back from Afghanistan. It was surreal to be sitting around a table smiling and joking around while preparing for the joint interviews that the Army had arranged.

Over a few beers later that night, Brink—the first soldier to spot the suicide bomber—pulled me aside to share that one of the soldiers in our group was still having a hard time speaking about the events of that day. After we asked the soldier how he was doing, he eventually decided not to participate in the next day's marathon interview session.

More than three years after the suicide bombing, my Army brother was still hurting deeply inside, which made sharing his story with strangers very difficult. It reminded me that so many combat veterans, including myself, grapple with these types of emotions on a daily basis.

The next day marked Veterans Day, which was a big blur of camera lights and microphones. From sunrise to sunset, we were peppered with question after question—individually and as a group—from reporters all around the globe. It was extremely taxing, and other than August 8, 2012, was more emotionally draining than any combat mission I had ever led.

That night, my soldiers and I got together to unwind, tell stories, and raise our glasses to the fallen. This time, we were joined by our boss, General Mingus, and his wife, Amy, which made the evening even more memorable.

On the morning of November 12, I woke up at 0700 to begin my day just like any other with a cup of coffee and fifty push-ups. The only difference was that this time I carefully put on a formal dress uniform.

Before Carsen and I walked out of our hotel room, I gave her a kiss.

"Today, our life might change in theory, but I will never change," I told her. "I love you more than anything in the world."

After putting on my coat, I looked in the mirror and smiled. I never wanted to be in this position, I thought, but here I was. As Heather Gray had told me when we first met, God had spared me and given me the tools to keep making a difference for families of the fallen and veterans. That meant I needed to devote my entire life to being a better person. In that quiet moment before heading to the White House, I accepted the challenge. A few minutes later, my one hundred guests and I boarded buses for a police escort through rush hour traffic to the White House.

As I sat alone on the bus, Carsen, who was sitting in front of me, turned around to make sure I was okay. Her compassionate eyes brought me back into the once-in-a-lifetime moment.

After several rounds of thorough screenings by White House security officials and the Secret Service, Carsen and I, along with our families, including her brother, Max, were taken to a beautiful green room of sorts to await further instructions. When that guidance was given, I barely paid attention, as I was too distracted by the intricate White House decor. Suddenly, I was a long way from a tiny forwarding operating base in Afghanistan or the inside of a hospital room.

This is really happening, I thought. *You can't turn around and leave.*

After a few more minutes of admiring the green room's historic artwork, my parents, Carsen, and I were suddenly whisked out of the room and into the West Wing. The president, we were told, would soon be in the Oval Office to meet with us.

I was excited to see President Obama again. Every time we had met or talked, he had always been so friendly. My sweaty palms met Carsen's as we waited outside the Oval Office.

My heart was racing by the time the giant white door opened. As usual, though, the tension disappeared as soon as I heard the president's voice.

"Flo!" he said while giving me a firm handshake. "It's great to see you again."

After welcoming me into the Oval Office, President Obama hugged Carsen and my mother before shaking my father's hand.

Then we walked toward his desk, where President Obama signed a certificate that made my Medal of Honor official. After signing, he got up and asked us to join him for a group picture.

The president then inquired where I was working, and how things had been going since the White House announced I would be receiving the Medal of Honor.

"Just trying to keep everything in perspective, Mr. President," I said. "Actually, I just finished painting Carsen's old apartment. She moved in this week."

Everyone laughed as we entered an elevator that would take us back to the green room.

As we prepared to walk into the East Room, I realized that I was standing to the president's right, which could be viewed by some as disrespectful to our country's leader and commander-in-chief.

"Sir, would you prefer that I walk to your left?" I asked President Obama.

"Don't worry about formalities," he said. "This is your day."

As I looked below the bright lights and into the audience, I saw Brink, Mahoney, Secor, Ochart, and Balderrama. I also appreciated that Jensen and McCain, the two soldiers who drove me from the blast site to the field hospital, were there. They were seated near General Mingus and his wife, along with my boss's brother, Shawn, and his wife, Karen.

In addition to Staley, my Afghanistan battle buddy and college classmate Saul Thompson was there, along with Army friends Hugh Miller, Tommy Anderson, John Wade, and Captain Jason McPhee (a different McPhee than the specialist I served with during my first deployment).

Retired Army Staff Sergeant Salvatore Giunta, who had received the Medal of Honor for heroism in Afghanistan nearly five years to the day before my ceremony, was sitting among the many past recipients in attendance. I was in awe of each and every one of them.

Sal had not only served as a mentor during the hectic days leading up to this moment, but had also fought alongside Staff Sergeant Erick Gallardo in the perilous Korengal Valley. In a bizarre, rather mind-boggling coincidence, Gallardo was the same soldier who encouraged me to get up and keep going when I thought about quitting Ranger School.

On the civilian side, Matt Sanders, who was in my hospital room at Walter Reed when the president came to visit, was joined by childhood friends Adam Forgione, Steve Carlin, Jamie Baker, and many others.

Whatever happiness I felt in seeing my friends vanished as soon as I looked back toward the Gold Star families, and specifically the children. Heather Gray had brought Nyah, eleven, Garrett, nine, and Ava, seven. When I looked at those sweet kids, all I could think about was running faster on August 8. If I could have pushed the suicide bomber to the ground one second earlier, maybe their dad would still be alive.

Pamela Griffin had brought Kevin's and her son, Dane, twenty-six, who had served with honor and distinction in Iraq, and their daughter, Kylie, nineteen.

Kami Kennedy brought Tom's and her five-year-old twins, Maggie and Brody. Also in attendance were Tom's parents, George and Patricia, his brothers, John and George Jr., and Kami's sister, Kitchi Joyce.

Each Gold Star wife appeared emotional by the end of the invocation and the start of President Obama's remarks.

"Good morning, and welcome to the White House," President Obama said. "A little more than three years ago, as Captain Florent Groberg was recovering from his wounds as a consequence of the actions that we honor today, he woke up on a hospital bed, in a little bit of a haze. He wasn't sure, but he thought he was in Germany, and someone was at his bedside talking to him.

"He thought it was the lead singer from the heavy metal band Korn," the president continued as the audience began to laugh. "Flo thought, 'What's going on? Am I hallucinating?' But he wasn't. It was all real.

"And so today, Flo, I want to assure you, you are not hallucinating," President Obama said with a grin. "You are actually in the White House. Those cameras are on. I am not the lead singer from Korn."

As the audience laughed even louder, I surprised myself by laughing, too. It felt good to see all the smiles in the East Room.

"We are here to award you our nation's highest military honor and distinction, the Medal of Honor," the president said.

Suddenly, I was embarrassed and uncomfortable once again. My leg was still hurting. Despite my awkwardness, the president proceeded to give an eloquent speech filled with honor, warmth, and humor.

Now, Flo and I have actually met before. Three years ago, I was on one of my regular visits to Walter Reed to spend some time with our wounded warriors—and Flo was one of them. We talked. It turns out he liked the Chicago Bears—so I liked him right away. And I had a chance to meet his parents who could not be more gracious and charming, and you get a sense of where Flo gets his character from. It is wonderful to see both of you again.

I also want to welcome Flo's girlfriend Carsen, who apparently, Flo tells me, he had to help paint an apartment with just the other day. So there's some honeydew lists going on.

Once again, there was laughter. When we met a little more than a year earlier, Carsen never could have imagined being recognized by the president as her boyfriend received the nation's highest military award.

Carsen had watched previous Medal of Honor ceremonies on YouTube and seen Presidents Obama, Bush, and their predecessors almost always mention the wives and fiancées in their speeches. Given that she was neither at the time, she never thought her name would be mentioned. She told me later that the fact that President Obama saw fit to mention her showed a genuine respect for our relationship and it meant a lot to her.

The president continued while I stood with my arms crossed; left hand over my right. Sweat was also beginning to drip from my chin and forehead.

His many friends, fellow soldiers and family, all of our distinguished guests: A day after Veterans Day, we honor this American veteran, whose story—like so many of our vets and wounded warriors—speaks not only of gallantry on the battlefield, but resilience here at home.

As a teenager just up the road in Bethesda, Flo discovered he had an incredible gift: he could run. Fast. Half-mile, mile, two mile: he'd leave his competition in the dust. He was among the best in the state. And he went on to run track and cross country at the University of Maryland.

Flo's college coach called him "the consummate teammate." As good as he was in individual events, somehow he always found a little extra something when he was running on a relay, with a team. Distance running is really all about guts—and as one teammate said, Flo could "suffer a little more than everyone else could." So day after day, month after month, he pushed himself to his limit. He knew that every long run, every sprint, every interval could help shave off a second or two off his times. And as he'd find out later, a few seconds can make all the difference.

I looked straight into the camera lights as the speech continued, but as soon as I heard the word "bomb" while President Obama told the story of that day, my nervous glance quickly moved downward toward the Gold Star families. For a split second, I locked eyes with Tom Kennedy's two brothers, whose eyes were welling up with tears.

The motorcycles had been a diversion. And at that moment, Flo did something extraordinary: he grabbed the bomber by his vest and kept pushing him away. And all those years of training on the track, in the classroom, out in the field, all of it came together. In those few seconds, he had the instincts and the courage to do what was needed. One of Flo's comrades, Sergeant Andrew Mahoney, had joined in, too, and together they shoved the bomber again and again. And they pushed him so hard he fell to the ground onto his chest. And then the bomb detonated.

Ball bearings, debris, dust exploded everywhere.

The increasing pain in my leg as I continued to stand was nothing compared to the discomfort I felt in watching three families—especially the children—listen to a story that ended with their loved ones being killed.

That blast by the bridge claimed four American heroes: four heroes Flo wants us to remember today. One of his mentors, a twenty-four-year Army vet who always found time for Flo and any other soldier who wanted to talk: Command Sergeant Major Kevin Griffin. A West Pointer who loved hockey and became a role model to cadets and troops because he always "cared more about other people than himself": Major Tom Kennedy. A popular Air Force leader known for smiling with his "whole face," someone who always seemed to run into a friend wherever he went: Major David Gray. And finally, a USAID foreign service officer who had just volunteered for a second tour in Afghanistan; a man who moved to the United States from Egypt and reveled in everything American, whether it was Disneyland or chain restaurants or roadside pie: Ragaei Abdelfattah.

These four men believed in America. They dedicated their lives to our country. They died serving it. Their families— loving wives and children, parents and siblings—bear that sacrifice most of all. So while Ragaei's family could not be with us today, I'd ask three Gold Star families to please stand and accept our deepest thanks.

This is your day, not mine, I thought while clapping for the Griffin, Gray, and Kennedy families during a burst of emotion that instantly swamped the East Room. I was also thinking about the Abdelfattah family, halfway across the world in Egypt.

By this point, tears were filling my eyes, sweat was readily apparent, and my nose had become obnoxiously runny, which my mom— bless her heart—noticed and signaled me to wipe.

Today, we honor Flo because his actions prevented an even greater catastrophe. You see, by pushing the bomber away from the formation, the explosion occurred farther from our forces, and on the ground instead of in the open air. And while Flo didn't know it at the time, that explosion also caused a second, unseen bomb to detonate before it was in place. Had both bombs gone off as planned, who knows how many could have been killed.

Those are the lives Flo helped to save. And we are honored that many of them are here today. Brigadier General James Mingus. Sergeant Andrew Mahoney, who was awarded a Silver Star for joining Flo in confronting the attacker. Sergeant First

Class Brian Brink, who was awarded a Bronze Star with Valor for pulling Flo from the road. Specialist Daniel Balderrama, the medic who helped to save Flo's leg. Private First Class Benjamin Secor and Sergeant Eric Ochart, who also served with distinction on that day. Gentlemen, I'd ask you to please stand and accept the thanks of a grateful nation, as well.

As soon as we finished applauding the real heroes of this story, I wanted the ceremony to end. I was in dire emotional and physical pain, and I didn't know how much more my tired mind and body could withstand.

At Walter Reed, Flo began his next mission: the mission to recover. He suffered significant nerve damage, and almost half of the calf muscle in his left leg had been blown off. So the leg that had powered him around that track, the leg that moved so swiftly to counter the bomber, that leg had been through hell and back. Thanks to thirty-three surgeries and some of the finest medical treatment a person can ask for, Flo kept that leg. He's not running, but he's doing a lot of CrossFit. I would not challenge him to CrossFit. He's putting some hurt on some rowing machines and some stair climbers. I think it is fair to say he is fit.

Today, Flo is medically retired. But like so many of his fellow veterans of our 9/11 Generation, Flo continues to serve. As I said yesterday at Arlington, that's what our veterans do: they are incredibly highly skilled, dynamic leaders always looking to write that next chapter of service to America. For Flo, that means a civilian job with the Department of Defense to help take care of our troops and keep our military strong.

And every day that he is serving, he will be wearing a bracelet on his wrist—as he is today—a bracelet that bears the names of his brothers in arms who gave their lives that day. The truth is, Flo says that day was the worst day of his life. And that is the stark reality behind these Medal of Honor ceremonies: that for all the valor we celebrate, and all the courage that inspires us, these actions were demanded amid some of the most dreadful moments of war.

That's precisely why we honor heroes like Flo, because on his very worst day, he managed to summon his very best. That's the nature of courage: not being unafraid, but confronting fear and danger and performing in a selfless fashion. He showed his guts, he showed his training; how he would put it all on the line for his teammates. That's an American we can all be grateful for. It's why we honor Captain Florent Groberg today.

May God bless all who serve and all who have given their lives to our country. We are free because of them. May God bless their families and may God continue to bless the United States of America with heroes such as these.

When I saw President Obama step away from the podium, I knew it was my cue to turn half right and give my back to the commander-in-chief, who would face forward while the official citation was read before placing the Medal of Honor around my neck.

As an Army major prepared to read the citation, my eyes focused on crystals adorning a chandelier hanging from the White House ceiling. I was exhausted, and as an imaginary blowtorch continued melting away my leg, I was preparing to collapse.

At the end of my rope, the president's military aide began reading aloud in a confident, booming voice.

This is it. I am going to fall down.

As my left leg turned in to Jell-O, I wasn't sure whether to tumble forward into the crowd or backward onto the president. With my mind clouded by fear and embarrassment, I decided that since

President Obama had been so nice to me and my family, he would understand if I fell into him.

"Captain Groberg's extraordinary heroism and selflessness above and beyond the call of duty at the risk of his life are in keeping with the highest traditions of the military service, and reflect great credit upon himself, Fourth Infantry Brigade Combat Team, Fourth Infantry Division, and the United States Army," the major said in conclusion.

Feeling the air shift ever so slightly behind me, I somehow managed to stay on my feet. Suddenly, I thought of my Uncle Abdou.

"You are my Flo," he would have said. *"I won't let anything happen to you."*

In an instant, a final burst of energy temporarily strengthened my wobbly left leg just in time for the president to put the medal in place.

After gently tapping my right shoulder to signal for me to turn around and face him, President Obama extended his hand.

"Good job, Flo," he said.

"Thank you, sir," I whispered back.

Together, we turned and faced the audience, all of whom rose up in applause. It was finally over, and I breathed a gigantic sigh of relief before looking into the eyes of my parents, Carsen, and the Griffins, Grays, and Kennedys. I gently nodded my head toward the Gold Star families to acknowledge that their loved ones had been memorialized for eternity at the White House.

After the benediction, President Obama made his closing remarks.

"That concludes the formal portion of this ceremony," the president said. "I need to take some pictures with the outstanding team members, as well as the Gold Star families who are here today, as Flo reminds us this medal, in his words, honors them as much as any honors that are bestowed upon him. And on Veterans Day Week, that is particularly appropriate."

He continued by thanking my fellow soldiers and jokingly reminding everyone that we were about to eat some "pretty decent" food prepared by the White House kitchen staff. This also got a laugh from the audience, and with that, the ceremony concluded.

It was the most trying twenty minutes of my life since August 8, 2012.

Millions of Americans watch a Medal of Honor ceremony on television thinking that it is a happy or even joyous occasion. For most soldiers, sailors, airmen, and Marines, it is in fact a devastating experience. We never wanted the Medal of Honor. We wanted to bring our battle buddies home to their parents, siblings, spouses, and children.

Before leaving the stage, I looked toward Dane and Kylie Griffin, along with five beautiful, much younger children: Nyah, Garrett, and Ava Gray, and Maggie and Brody Kennedy. I said to myself, I will never forget your fathers. Our country will never forget them. Every time I look at my medal, I see their faces, and yours.

While humbled by the Medal of Honor's significance and the responsibility it carries, the greatest honor of my life will always be having served beside heroes like Command Sergeant Major Kevin Griffin, Major Tom Kennedy, Major David Gray, and Foreign Service Officer Ragaei Abdelfattah.

When my time comes, I cannot wait to see you guys again.

EPILOGUE THE NEXT MISSION

After the Medal of Honor ceremony, I followed President Obama back into the green room, where the president, the Gold Star families, and I took dozens of pictures together.

One moment I will always treasure from that day was watching the president play Rock, Paper, Scissors with David and Heather Gray's kids. The smiles on Nyah's, Garrett's, and Ava's faces—along with Heather's and mine—lit up the room.

Once our pictures were taken, President Obama said goodbye and retired back to the Oval Office while I played guest of honor at the reception, where I was finally able to sit and rest my aching leg. I probably took over five hundred pictures and shook just as many hands over the next couple of hours.

After we left the White House, I went back to the hotel and had a few drinks with my closest friends and family. I was relieved that the day was over while also beginning to truly appreciate its full significance.

I was not only a recipient of the Medal of Honor, but had just become a member of one of the world's most exclusive societies. At the same time, I was still Flo. I didn't grow any wings or become wiser; I was now just responsible for much more.

The following day, I spoke at a Pentagon auditorium in front of our nation's military leaders, including the Secretary of Defense, Ash Carter. I must admit that I was nervous to be inducted into the Pentagon's storied Hall of Heroes, but I spoke from the heart while highlighting fellow American soldiers who meant the world to me, including my entire August 8, 2012, team, General James Mingus, and SFC Korey Staley.

"Today I stand in front of you as a proud American, grateful to have been given the opportunity to serve and wear the colors for our country in a time of war," I began. "I was blessed to be surrounded, trained, mentored, led, and followed by some of our nation's greatest warriors."

Early in the speech, I asked SFC Staley to stand up. After the audience applauded, I told them how much his guidance meant to me during those very first days in Afghanistan.

"He talked to me. He listened to me. He taught me," I said while looking toward Staley. "He was the NCO you need as a young officer in order to become successful. Most importantly, he allowed me to be the right leader at that time to bring home our boys."

Next, I turned to SFC Brian Brink, for whom the audience also applauded.

"He was there with me—to my right, to my left, in front of me, to the rear—at all times," I said of Brink before offering my sincere thanks.

Later in the speech, the audience applauded the rest of my August 8, 2012, teammates when I asked them to stand and be recognized. It was a special moment that they richly deserved, as I told the Pentagon audience.

When you deploy and you're in combat, these individuals become your brothers and you will do anything for them. And you all are.

Mahoney . . . I never had to worry about Mahoney. Mahoney squared me away quite a few times. He was sarcastic at times; a typical sergeant who looks at a lieutenant. You'd ask him to do something and he'd do it with a little smirk.

I had Balderrama, who I owe my life to, as well as with Brink. Balderrama saved my life. Simple. I would have died that day. I was bleeding out. He kept me awake; he gave me a tourniquet. For that, I can't even say thank you. That's not enough.

Secor and Ochart. PFCs. Unbelievable. Guys who go into Afghanistan young and so proud, and you tell them "Hey, I need you to do this." On that day, I switched everything. I told Ochart "Hey, you're no longer at the top of the diamond, you're at the rear of the diamond, and if something happens, you take the colonel down and you take him to safety. I don't care what he says to you. You are the boss now." And all he said was "Roger that, sir." And he did that.

Secor. "Hey Secor, I'm going to need you to move to the front with Brink even though the entire tour you've been next to Command Sergeant Major Griffin." He looked at me, didn't like it, and he said "Roger that, sir." And he moved up there.

I am so proud of you guys. It's an honor to have served with you. And you are brothers for life, and I love you guys.

Last, but certainly not least, I thanked the boss.

"The way he led made everyone want to be better," I said of General Mingus, who was in attendance. "His personality made our job easy.

"I would have and still would, lay down my life for you, sir," I continued. "Thank you."

When I said the names of our four fallen brothers, their names echoed through the Pentagon's Hall of Heroes.

On August 8, 2012, our country lost four incredible Americans. Four men who made the ultimate sacrifice. Four individuals who changed lives around them for the better. Four true heroes for which this Medal of Honor belongs. I carry it in my heart, I carry it on my body, I carry it in my soul every single day. I miss them and I understand that my responsibility in this world is to now live through them and live for them and their families, and to be better.

Just like the day before at the White House, the audience clapped for the Griffin, Gray, and Kennedy families, as well as the Abdelfattahs, who were always in our hearts.

"The biggest fear I always had when I came back from Afghanistan—I had two," I said to the Gold Star families. "First was that you would not accept me because I was not able to bring everyone home."

I then turned to General Mingus.

"And second, that I could no longer do my job and bring you home, sir," I said to my boss. "I wanted that job and I wanted to be there until December but I couldn't do it anymore. These were the two demons I lived with."

Turning back to the families, I dug even deeper to speak from my soul.

But what you represent, the Gold Star families, is everything of what America is. Though I'm here today and your loved ones are not, they are here in spirit with us. They are in my heart, they are in every one of my guys' hearts, every single person who was involved that day, they are with them and their families. But you still came to support us, you still came to support me, and you still came to support each other. This honor is yours. All yours. This medal: I carry on my body, but it is yours. It is for you. And I mean it from everything inside of me.

Holding off tears, I took another deep breath, strengthened my resolve, and was ultimately able to finish my remarks.

"Thank you for being you," I said to the Griffins, Grays, and Kennedys. "And I love you."

And then, just like that, it was all over.

I soon retreated to my room, packed my belongings, and went home with Carsen. We spent the night at home before we took off the next day for a monthlong Medal of Honor tour across several American cities.

Our first stop was New York, where I rang the bell at the New York Stock Exchange and made an appearance on *The Late Show with Stephen Colbert*. Our next stops were Chicago, where I joined the *Steve Harvey* show, and then Los Angeles for a segment on the NFL Network.

During the trip, we started every morning at 5:30 with appearances on different news programs such as *Fox & Friends* and *Morning Joe*. During the day we would visit the NYPD, FDNY, World Trade Center, Chicago Police Department, the Anaheim Fire Department, and many more. Those visits meant so much to me and ended up being the highlight of my travels because I got to spend time with some of our country's finest, who generally do not get the same credit as those who serve in the military. They should.

During this trip, I connected with some dear, lifelong friends, including Eric Fanning, Ben Masri-Cohen, Robert Couture, Tamara Young, Tony Mottola, John Glotzbach, Pablo Araya, and Adam Gase. I also began to truly understand what the Medal of Honor meant to so many people. The responsibility was real and seemed daunting at times, but this was part of my new reality. I embraced it.

I had the opportunity to close my travels with a few days back in Colorado Springs visiting the troops at Fort Carson and spending time with the Mingus and Griffin families. Being so close to Christmas, this trip meant a lot to me.

Following the holidays, I went back to work for the Department of Defense. Though I was no longer in the position that I previously held because of the prominent nature of the Medal of Honor ceremonies and media exposure, it felt good to be back at work with a daily routine.

Over the course of the following months, I noticed that I had an opportunity to make a deep impact in the community by bringing awareness to the problems our veterans and their families face when they transition out of the military and back into civilian society. Therefore, I partnered with my good friend Greg Call, who led the veterans mission at LinkedIn, to embark on an amazing year-long ride. With the help of Dan Savage, Nick Bartle, and Joshua Mitchell, we created numerous commercials, campaigns, and educational videos highlighting our veteran community and what vets bring to corporate America and the education sector. I also wrote quite a few articles about my struggles and what led to my success.

Today, Greg works for Amazon, Nick works for Pandora, and Dan is leading the veterans mission at LinkedIn. I'm glad to know our work will continue to impact all of these companies, and more, as we continue pursuing our careers.

Although not what I expected to be doing, my new career is a blessing. I am now a member of the Boeing Company, where I am part of a team that consists of more than 22,000 self-identified veterans. Since joining the company, I have been amazed at how much time our employees—veterans and civilians alike—spend in our local communities.

Through programs and partnerships with great organizations like the National Park Service, the USO, The Mission Continues, and RP/6 (now USO Transition Services), Boeing and its employees are driving positive, lasting change for our military and all who have served.

Part of the Boeing mission is to protect our troops by providing them with the best equipment the industry can offer in order to safely and successfully accomplish the mission. My mission is to ensure that members of our military, veterans, and their families are taken care of back home. We accomplish this through programs that focus on transition, health, wellness, and volunteering, because we at Boeing know that this country will only continue to grow and prosper with our veterans helping to lead the way.

ACKNOWLEDGMENTS
Flo Groberg

I would like to thank all my friends and family who supported me before and after August 8, 2012. Foremost, I want to thank Saul, Sanders, and Brendan, who supported me throughout my recovery.

I also want to mention my cousin Anthony, who is currently serving in the army of my native country, France.

I want to send all my love to my mom and dad for always being there for me, whether in person or in spirit. My mom dedicated her life to me to make sure I would be successful. She loved me from first sight and I know that she would do anything for me. As a son that is the greatest gift you could ever ask for.

My father is my hero. He sacrificed so much to make sure that I would succeed in this world. He advised me and occasionally let me fail, but was always there to give me a leg up. He has always loved me, and though he wasn't created to demonstrate his feelings, he let me know anytime I ever needed it. He made me a man, and I consider him the greatest person that a boy could have asked for as a father.

ACKNOWLEDGMENTS

To Carsen, the woman who has stood by my side since our first date in October of 2014: Thank you for your support, unconditional love, and your strength. I could never repay you for what you have done for me when nobody was around to witness. You are my heart and soul. It is a fact that my life wouldn't be this fruitful or joyful without you in it. You have closed gaps and opened my eyes to a whole new perspective. Today, I feel like the luckiest man in the world to be by your side. I still can't believe that you accepted me so quickly and without any reservations when I proposed to you on December 28, 2016.

Lastly, Carsen, I want to applaud you and thank you for all the work that you put into this book. You spent a lot of time analyzing, correcting, rewriting, and supporting *8 Seconds of Courage*. It is only through your incredible talent and vision that my memories and feelings have been transformed into words. I love you.

I do not consider myself a hero: I'm an American soldier who transitioned back as a civilian. Yes, I did receive the Medal of Honor, but it does not belong to me. I am merely a courier. The medal represents our nation's finest individuals who made the ultimate sacrifice for our way of life, for our freedom. The medal represents the Gold Star families who must live with the consequences of a loved one who did not come home. This medal belongs to the United States of America—the greatest country in the world, day in and day out. This medal belongs to you. God bless our military and God bless America.

Hooah.

ACKNOWLEDGMENTS
Tom Sileo

I vividly remember watching retired Captain Florent Groberg receive the Medal of Honor on the small TV in my home office. During President Obama's speech, I was struck not only by Flo's courage, but by the emphasis he had asked the president to place on telling the stories of his four fallen brothers.

Ten weeks later, I decided to send Flo a direct message on Twitter. To be honest, I did not expect a reply, especially in the Medal of Honor ceremony's whirlwind aftermath.

I was wrong. After just three hours, Flo replied with his phone number. During our subsequent conversation, we arranged to meet for dinner in Washington, D.C., where we would be joined by Flo's wonderful girlfriend (and now fiancée), Carsen.

When we shook hands, I noticed that Flo was wearing the bracelet honoring his fallen teammates. As soon as we started discussing the possibility of writing a book, however, I realized that the bracelet wasn't only on his wrist. It was wrapped around his heart.

ACKNOWLEDGMENTS

Before we finished dinner on that February night, Flo, Carsen, and I raised our glasses in honor of Kevin Griffin, David Gray, Tom Kennedy, Ragaei Abdelfattah, and their families. Soon after, we started working on *8 Seconds of Courage*.

Flo, I can never thank you enough for trusting me to help you tell this incredible story. Every day, you inspire me by being so selfless and humble in carrying out your life's new mission to honor the fallen. My daughter will grow up learning about American heroes like you, Kevin, David, Tom, Ragaei, and your families.

Carsen, I deeply appreciate your enormous contributions to this book. You are a talented writer, vigilant editor, and devoted fiancée to Flo. Congratulations on your engagement!

Thank you to my loving and extremely patient wife, Lisa. As with the first two books, you encouraged me every step of the way, especially during those many months that I spent away from you and our beautiful daughter, Reagan. I love you both!

To my father, Bob, my mother, Diane, her husband, Bruce, my sister, Lauren, and her husband, Mark: Thanks for letting me stay in your respective homes while I was in town working with Flo.

To our phenomenal agent, E. J. McCarthy, thank you for your expert guidance and your faith in me. I look forward to working with you on a fourth book and spending many more hours on the phone talking baseball. You are the best!

To Bob Bender and the entire Simon & Schuster team, thanks for believing in Flo's story. Working with you has been a privilege.

Most of all, I want to thank the Griffin, Gray, Kennedy, and Abdelfattah families, along with the many Gold Star spouses, parents, siblings, and children who have been willing to share their emotional stories with me through the years. Your strength is a constant source of motivation. Until my last breath, I will do everything I can to spotlight the heroism of your loved ones. Because of them and you, our country is free.

INDEX

INDEX

INDEX

INDEX

INDEX

INDEX

INDEX

INDEX

INDEX

INDEX

INDEX